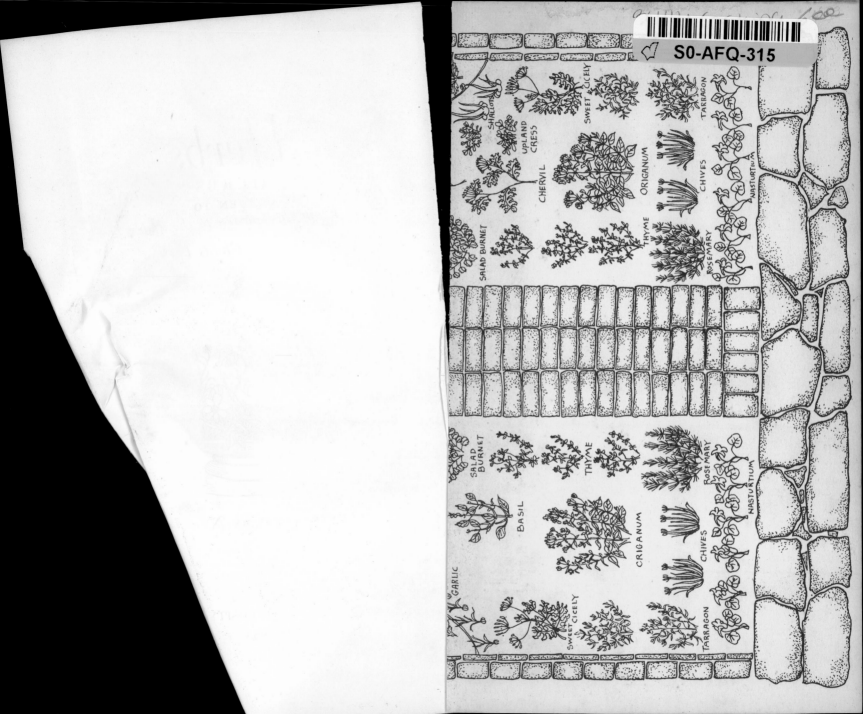

HERBS

From the Garden to the Table

Herbs

FROM THE GARDEN TO THE TABLE

BY *Dorothy Childs Hogner*

ILLUSTRATIONS BY *Nils Hogner*

New York
OXFORD UNIVERSITY PRESS
1953

PRINTED IN THE UNITED STATES OF AMERICA

'*And God said, Behold,*
I have given you every herb bearing seed,
which is upon the face of all the earth.'

GEN. 1:29

Contents

Introduction

WE HAVE BEEN MOTIVATED to write this book by our belief that everyone who has a garden will delight, as we do, in the experience of growing, harvesting, and using their own herbs. As we sit in our country studio, the heady fragrance of thyme, dill, lovage, marjoram, tarragon, and other herbs is mingled with the wood smoke from the open fire, creating an almost narcotic incense, soothing to anyone in the least inclined to suffer from the tension of modern life. In our desire to revive the use of herbs so well known to our great grand-parents, we have no intention of dispelling the mystery which surrounds herb lore. Herbs have a history as old as man himself. They are identified with the beginnings of civilization. However, we do wish to terminate the belief that herbs are plants reserved for use by a selected, initiated few. Herbs were formerly used by Everyman and so they will be used again today.

This then is the purpose of our book: to introduce the person who likes to prepare food to a fundamental knowledge of the plants that can help the cook achieve a gourmet's satisfaction. Although there are herb books in print, some of which are very old and available only in the original editions in libraries, and others on the market that are modern or are reprints, we feel strongly that there is a need for a practical book that explains how to apply up-to-date methods of gardening to a garden of ancient herbs, and one, furthermore, that supplies the key to cooking with herbs. With this in mind, we offer a small herbal with the stress on the twenty-four basic culinary herbs, information on growing, harvesting, and cooking with these, and additional information on many culinary, medicinal, industrial, and scent herbs.

The gardening and culinary information in this book is from our own personal experience. We grow all the herbs described with one exception, the sweet bay tree, *Laurus nobilis*.

ACKNOWLEDGMENTS

FOR ASSISTANCE in gathering material on the history of herbs, and for advice on technical matters of horticulture and problems relating to regional data, we are indebted to many people. We are very grateful to Miss E. C. Hall, librarian of The New York Botanical Garden, and Mrs. E. Enid Grote, librarian of The Horticultural Society of New York for their unfailing courtesy and assistance in making available to us originals of important old herbals such as Gerard's, and the Oxford edition (now out of print) of Gunther's Dioscorides. In quite another field, we are indebted to Dr. C. Loyal W. Swanson, Head of the Department of Soils, the Connecticut Agricultural Experiment Station, for help in preparing the section on soils; to Neely Turner, Chief of the Department of Entomology at the Connecticut Station, for help with information on insect pests; to J. C. Krysl and C. H. Phillips, Bureau of Entomology and Plant Quarantine, the United States Department of Agriculture, for help on material concerning registration of a nursery; to Miss Elsie Taylor, reference division of the British Information Services, for checking information on the Royal Maundy; and, for data on mint production, to Richard M. Perry, Department of Agriculture, Olympia, Washington, Genevieve Morgan, State Department of Agriculture, Salem, Oregon, N. K. Ellis, Head Department of Horticulture, Purdue University, Indiana, and Paul M. Harmer, Muck Soil Specialist, State of Michigan.

We wish to thank the directors and sponsors of the botanical gardens listed in the appendix for answering a questionnaire on herb gardens, and, in particular, the following who gave us invaluable data on regional growing problems: Forest J. Goodrich, Dean of the College of Pharmacy, University of Washington, Seattle; Tracey G. Call, Associate Professor Pharma-

cognosy, Montana State University; Mrs. Janet Wright, Assist-
ant to the curator emeritus, Henry E. Huntington Library and
Art Gallery, and Botanical gardens, San Marino, California;
H. Teuscher, curator, Montreal Botanical Garden, Canada;
Carl H. Johnson, College of Pharmacy, University of Florida;
Egil Ramstad, School of Pharmacy, Purdue University, Indiana;
W. R. Brewer, College of Pharmacy, University of Arizona;
Edgar Anderson, Missouri Botanical Garden; Dr. H. R. Totten,
Botany Department, Chapel Hill, North Carolina; Miss Emma
B. Richardson, The Heyward-Washington House Garden,
Charleston, South Carolina; the directors of the Indiana Botanic
Garden, Hammond, Indiana; the directors of the John Blair
Herb Garden and Wythe Herb Garden, Colonial Williams-
burg, Virginia; Dr. Kenneth Redman, Professor of Pharma-
cognosy, South Dakota State College of Agriculture; Miss Leila
Compton, Wooster, Ohio; Henry M. Burlage, Dean, The Uni-
versity of Texas; Dr. C. C. Albers, Professor of Pharmacognosy,
The University of Texas.

To Gordon Waaser, of F. P. Garrettson Company, Baldwin,
Long Island; and Charles O. Ruegger Jr. and John Cavarro,
of Bazar Francais, 666 Sixth Avenue, New York City, we are
indebted for information on marketing food products to the
gourmet shops.

Among many others who have answered our innumerable
questions are T. H. Everett, Horticulturist, The New York
Botanical Garden; Robert B. Fisher, Horticulturist, Mount
Vernon Ladies' Association of the Union; Esther Ann Huebner,
Gardener, The Cloisters, The Metropolitan Museum of Art;
Raymond P. Atherton, Agricultural Agent, Litchfield, Connec-
ticut; W. C. Muenscher, Cornell University; Dorcas Brigham,
Village Hill Nursery, Massachusetts. We are especially indebted
to the members of The Herb Society of America for help and
inspiration in this field in which they have pioneered in modern
times, with a special word of thanks to Mrs. Frances R.
Williams.

HERBS

From the Garden to the Table

1

The Kitchen Herb Garden

'Though your Garden for flowers doth in a sort peculiarly challenge to itself a perfect, and exquisite form to the eyes, yet you may not altogether neglect this, where your herbs for the pot do grow.'

The Country House-wives Garden, William Lawson, 1617.

IN COLONIAL DAYS, garden thyme and aromatic sage, rosemary and sweet marjoram, and all species of herbs grown for their flavor were called sweet herbs. These, and others called potherbs which were commonly cooked as vegetables, include leaf herbs excellent for the salad bowl. It is in a kitchen herb garden of the ancient sweet herbs and potherbs that the modern cook can best learn to know the plants used in former days by Everyman in the preparation of fine foods; and, contrary to the belief of those who are unfamiliar with herbs, they are as easy to grow as garden vegetables and flowers. Successful commercial growers agree that anyone who can raise a good crop of carrots, lettuce, and tomatoes or a border of phlox and delphiniums will be successful in growing a garden of herbs.

Just as there are fundamental requirements necessary for vegetable gardening and for maintaining an attractive herbaceous border, however, so too there are special requirements for growing savory herbs. Nearly all those seen in kitchen gardens in America today are hundreds of generations away from their native home, many of them having come originally from the Mediterranean region where the soil is good, and alkaline, or in colloquial language 'sweet.' The soil in this region is lime-stone, Terra Rossa (red soil), and the climate warm temperate.

Location of Garden

Drainage is the most important single factor in choosing a spot for growing herbs. Good drainage is essential, even with the moisture-loving plants such as the mints. An obvious exception is the aquatic herb, water cress, but in general most herbs need a spot where puddles do not stand long after rain. A gentle slope is the best location for an herb garden, unless there is natural good drainage due to the porous character of the sub-soil, in which case level ground is preferable. Flat land that is boggy can be drained by ditching or by replacing with a layer of porous material, coarse gravel or coal cinders, the hard subsoil to a depth of about one foot, and topping this with a layer of good sandy loam.

In Elizabethan days, most herb gardens had good drainage because they were raised above the ground level; the soil was built up and confined by boards or other material, some of it quite exotic such as bones. Today boards treated with creosote or bricks are recommended for laying out this type of herb garden.

The second factor to consider in choosing a location is sunlight. Most herbs like to bask in the sun. The few exceptions that do better in shade will be noted under specific directions in the text.

Soil

Good soil is essential for propagating aromatic herbs. Like vegetables and flowers, herbs may survive in poor soil but they will not grow the way herbs should that are to be used as flavoring in your favorite recipe. Herbs grow so slowly in poor soil that the leaves are too tough for the salad bowl, and the flavor is often bitter. Therefore, in order to grow savory herbs, it is first necessary to study the structure of your soil, which is not mere dirt. Topsoil, or garden soil, is composed of decayed vegetable matter mixed with some decaying animal matter, pulverized rock (sand, clay, silt), and water carrying in solution certain chemicals, the lack of which will cause green leaves to turn yellow, become spotty, brown, and withered, and will stunt a plant's growth so that it is weakened and subject to disease.

The next time you walk in your garden, pick up a handful of earth, the food that, in combination with sunshine, air, and rain, will make your garden of herbs. Compress the earth in your hand, let it drop to the ground. A good friable loam, one that crumbles easily, is the quality of soil best suited to growing herbs. If you live in a section where the natural soil is clay or a sandy, heavy loam, the first thing to do is to lighten the soil, or improve its structure. Like most plants, herbs do poorly when the tilth (workability) of the soil is poor. The best method of improving the tilth is by adding humus, the organic material, partially or wholly decayed, commonly applied to gardens in the form of barn manure or compost. Humus will improve any heavy soil by lightening its structure which in turn will prevent water from running off the surface and thus permit moisture to penetrate to the herb roots; conversely, in a too sandy soil, humus will add substance and body and stop the water from percolating through the garden and leaching away the nutrients. Second, humus brings fertility to a barren land by adding plant foods. Humus is a source of several elements, particularly nitrogen, without which no plant—vegetable, flower, or herb—can grow or reproduce itself.

As to the nitrogen necessary for an herb garden, there must be enough to maintain a good *steady* growth. A lush leaf growth is undesirable because this does not proportionately increase the yield of essential oils, the volatile oils that give the aromatic flavor and sweet fragrance to herb products, but even less desirable is slow, stunted growth. Humus in the form of cow manure, compost, or a similar organic matter must be used in preparing the soil for the herb garden, and, unless the soil is naturally alkaline, it is also necessary to add lime.

Details on the best kinds of fertilizer, both organic and commercial, lime, and other elements necessary for maintaining an aromatic herb garden are discussed in Chapter 2, but in these first few paragraphs the reader has the basic information necessary for preparing the ground for a garden of herbs. Specific data on laying out the garden follow.

Size of Garden

An herb garden need not be large, nor is it necessary to grow most herbs in a special garden by themselves. Anyone who has a few feet of land can set out plants of at least three perennials, such as tarragon, thyme, and chives, and three short rows of the herbs easily raised from seed—for example, sweet marjoram, basil, and parsley—either in the vegetable garden, the flower border, or in a small bed at the kitchen door. The half dozen herbs listed above are both decorative and essential to the cook and will supply a tang to many different dishes. Once a gourmet has had an opportunity to use a few leaves of sweet herbs picked fresh from his own garden, he will not be satisfied with a mere half dozen herbs. A complete garden of culinary herbs must contain a minimum of twenty-four basic kinds.

THE TWENTY-FOUR BASIC KITCHEN HERBS

Balm, Lemon (*Melissa officinalis*)
Basil (*Ocimum Basilicum*)
Borage (*Borago officinalis*)
Burnet, Salad (*Sanguisorba minor*)
Chervil (*Anthriscus Cerefolium*)
Chives (*Allium Schoenoprasum*)
Cicely, Sweet (*Myrrhis odorata*)
Costmary (*Chrysanthemum Balsamita*)
Cress, Upland (*Barbarea praecox*)
Dill (*Anethum graveolens*)
Garlic (*Allium sativum*)
Lovage (*Levisticum officinale*)
Marjoram, Sweet (*Majorana hortensis*)
Mint (*Mentha spicata*)
Nasturtiums (*Tropaeolum minus*)
Origanum (*Origanum vulgare*— English variety)
Parsley (*Petroselinum hortense*)
Pennyroyal (*Mentha Pulegium*)
Rosemary (*Rosmarinus officinalis*)
Sage (*Salvia officinalis*)
Savory, Summer (*Satureia hortensis*)
Shallots (*Allium ascalonicum*)
Tarragon (*Artemisia Dracunculus*)
Thyme, Garden (*Thymus vulgaris*)

The space required for growing these two dozen herbs is surprisingly small. Because the flavor of herbs is so strong, a very

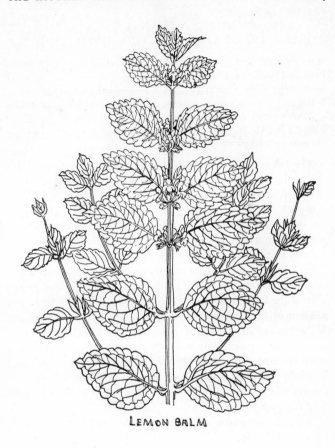

LEMON BALM

few plants of each will supply a cook with more green herbs than can be used in preparing meals. There will be enough left over to dry, and others from which to make aromatic vinegars. The plan shown is for a garden large enough to grow the basic twenty-four.

A PLAN
FOR A DECORATIVE KITCHEN HERB GARDEN

Size: 12′ x 14′
Path and border: 241 bricks
Restraining wall: 2 pieces (54″ x 9″) galvanized tin roofing
Fertilizer: 4 bushels barn manure, or 4 bushels compost, or 18 lbs.
   (commercial) dried cow manure
Lime: 2 lbs. (hydrated or agricultural)
Design: see end paper

The twenty-four basic herbs in the attractive kitchen garden design in the end paper are arranged according to height at maturity, nature of growth (whether tall or short, spreading or upright), length of life, and frost resistance. Herbs such as parsley that remain green late in the fall and winter over even in sub-zero climates offset those such as basil that complete their natural cycle in a few months, or die with the first frost.

It is easier to prepare the ground before you lay the path and border. Stake out the plot, 12 feet by 14 feet, and then, preferably in the fall, spread on the organic matter and the lime. The amount of fertilizer and lime given above is approximate and is for ground already in use as a garden in a region where the soil is a fairly good sandy loam. Of course, more organic matter must be used if the soil is heavy and the tilth poor, and, in a naturally alkaline region, lime would be omitted. The only certain way to determine the needs of a soil is to have it tested (see Chapter 2).

Turn the organic matter well under by spading deep, which, like the principle of deep plowing a larger garden, not only mixes the fertilizer with the soil but brings up minerals necessary to the life of plants. After the soil is spaded, then rake level and, using a string for a guide, lay out the center path three bricks wide. This will take 117 of the bricks and the remainder will complete the border, with one brick set edgewise and the other flat (see design). Next, sink the two pieces of galvanized sheet metal, one on each side of the garden to confine the mint and costmary. Set the metal snugly in a trench

deep enough to cover all but an inch of the top, one in each
of the two spaces of the center border, shown on diagram.
Unless the garden is surrounded by a lawn, in which case the
lawnmower will keep the mint from spreading on the grass side,
it may be necessary to sink another piece of metal on the outer
border behind the mint.

Now the garden is ready for planting.

GENERAL INSTRUCTIONS FOR PLANTING

The herbs that should be raised from seed are identified,
under the specific instructions on each herb. In general, plant
herb seeds as deep as four times the diameter of the seeds,
which for the smallest among the basic herbs, sweet marjoram,
means covering with only a mere sprinkle of earth. Then press
down with the hoe. Large seeds, such as sweet cicely, require
a furrow in the earth a quarter of an inch deep. If the weather
is dry, water the seed bed to hasten germination.

Standard procedure for setting out plants is to work in the
evening after the hot sun is gone, or on a cloudy day; dig a
hole large enough so as not to disturb the ball of earth around
the roots, and deep enough to accommodate the roots but not
to cover the crown. Fill the hole with water and let it drain
away before setting the plant; then fill the hole with soil, tamp
firmly around the roots, and finally scatter loose dry soil on the
surface as a mulch. Water every evening until the roots are
established. If the plants you buy are packed without earth,
prepare a hole large enough to spread the roots in a natural
position. Do not cramp them. Fill the hole with water, set the
plant in the hole, and let the roots soak while the water drains
away. Then proceed as above.

Details on growing each of the twenty-four basic herbs follow,
with notes on height, spacing, whether annual or perennial, and
the quantity of seeds or number of plants to buy for a garden
12 feet by 14 feet in area. These are the basic herbs used in the
recipes in Chapter 5.

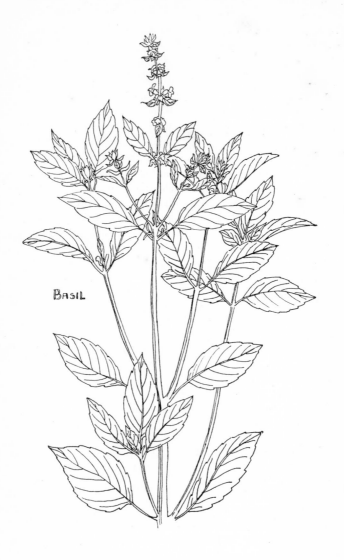

BASIL

HARDY PERENNIAL

Balm, Lemon (*Melissa officinalis*)   SELF-SOWS

2 plants (or 1 package of seeds)   SUB-ZERO WINTERS

Lemon balm is a hardy, herbaceous, perennial sweet herb, which withstands light frost but dies to the roots when freezing weather comes. Each spring the plant bears a bushy mass of pretty, lemon-scented, yellowish-green leaves, and some time later, small, inconspicuous yellow or whitish flowers.

Lemon balm likes full sun. It may be grown easily from seed, and if allowed to flower and set seed will self-sow generously. Two nursery plants will assure a crop of leaves the first season.

Seedlings should be set 18 inches apart. Plants will need that much space on all sides, and will grow about 2 feet tall. Lemon balm can be propagated by root division of old plants in early spring.

Basil, Sweet (*Ocimum Basilicum*)   ANNUAL

1 package of seeds   FROST-FREE MONTHS ONLY

Basil is an annual sweet herb, easily grown from seed sown after all danger of frost is past. The seedlings should be thinned to stand 8 inches apart, for each plant will need that much space at maturity. At a height of about 18 inches, basil will bear spikes of inconspicuous white flowers above a mass of aromatic, light green leaves.

To assure a second crop before frost, cut basil before the buds are open. Pinch back the tops of young plants to encourage a bushy growth.

The leaves of basil, like those of tomatoes and squash, are affected by the slightest frost, and with the first killing frost the whole plant withers and turns black.

There are several species and varieties of basil, all edible. Among them are the showy purple basil and the curly-leafed lettuce basil; sweet basil has the best flavor.

Borage (*Borago officinalis*)
1 package of seeds

HARDY ANNUAL
SELF-SOWS
TEMPERATE ZONE

Borage—pronounced to rhyme with either courage or porridge—the salad and stirrup-cup herb, is easily grown from seed sown in the spring as soon as the ground can be worked; and once established, borage will self-sow year after year. In our garden, one package of seeds planted more than a decade ago has produced hundreds of descendants. Soon after the ground thaws in spring in the area surrounding the place where borage has been seeded before, trim tender little borage leaves sprout in small nooks and corners. If taken very young, seedlings can be transplanted, but older plants are difficult to move because borage has a long tap root.

When young, borage is of modest size but presently the plants send out a sprawling growth, the leaves, oblong and oval, and very rough and hairy, growing larger and larger, with racemes of enchanting, delicately formed, azure blue or pale reddish-lavender, star-shaped flowers. The plants remain in continuous bloom all summer long and until the first frost when they are quickly reduced to a mass of blackened herbage, suitable only for the compost pile.

Borage grows luxuriantly. A mature plant will be 3 feet tall, perhaps taller, and will need at least 2 square feet of garden space.

Burnet, Salad (*Sanguisorba minor*)
2 plants (or 1 package of seeds)

HARDY PERENNIAL
SELF-SOWS
SUB-ZERO WINTERS

Salad burnet is easy to grow from seed sown in the spring as soon as the ground can be worked, but if in the first year the gardener wants to be assured of having the leaves for early summer salads, he must start with plants. If salad burnet is allowed to go to seed, it will self-sow. Of importance to the northern gardener is the fact that the leaves that grow close to the ground usually stay green all winter.

The pretty, feather-formed leaves are always tender, usually

BORAGE

glabrous, and sometimes very slightly hairy. They present a lacy effect, and the decorative quality is heightened when the slight, reddish stems rise up a foot, sometimes two, sometimes a little higher, and produce small roundish or oblong flower heads dotted with tiny white or rosy flowers. The effect somehow reminds one of miniature pineapples.

Allow about a square foot of space for each plant.

Chervil (*Anthriscus Cerefolium*)
1 package of seeds

HARDY ANNUAL
SELF-SOWS
TEMPERATE ZONE

This annual, aromatic sweet herb bears a slight resemblance to its cousin, parsley, but the leaves are more lacy and fern-like, and lighter green in color.

Sow chervil in early spring in semi-shade if possible. This native of the Caucasus region in western Asia needs some shade during the heat of summer. The leaves often burn in full sun.

The flowers of chervil are delicate white umbels, reminding one somewhat of Queen Anne's Lace, only smaller. When in flower, chervil plants measure 2 feet in height. If a gardener wishes a second, and possibly a third cutting, chervil should not be permitted to blossom. Cut it, and it will grow a new leaf crop, and will continue to grow after the first frost and until freezing weather comes.

Thin chervil plants so that they are about 6 inches apart.

Cicely, Sweet (*Myrrhis odorata*)
Giant Sweet Chervil
2 plants

HARDY PERENNIAL
SELF-SOWS
SUB-ZERO WINTERS

Sweet cicely, sometimes called giant sweet chervil but not to be confused with true chervil (*Anthriscus Cerefolium*), is a hardy, herbaceous perennial that can withstand some frost but dies to the ground in freezing weather. It is a sweet herb, salad, and potherb. The small white umbels of flowers are pretty, but even more so is the foliage, with its downy-haired fern-like leaves. Old plants present a decorative lacy green mass up to 3 feet high, and plants that are cut from time to time for their leaves, will need at least 1½ foot space per plant.

Buy 2 plants to make sure of a good growth the first year, but thereafter you will have a natural increase, for sweet cicely self-sows. The hard, ridged, brown-black seeds are seven-eighths of an inch long; they germinate slowly, often not at all if kept out of ground all winter, but if you gather ripe seeds before they drop and plant them by Labor Day, you will be sure of a crop of spring seedlings.

Sweet cicely may also be propagated by root division. In early spring when the first green leaves break through the ground, dig out one of the big, thick, fragrant roots and slice it with a sharp knife into two or more parts, leaving an eye to each piece; replant, in semi-shade if possible. Like the leaves of chervil, the leaves of sweet cicely may burn in full sun.

Chives (*Allium Schoenoprasum*)   HARDY PERENNIAL
2 plants   SUB-ZERO WINTERS

Chives are among the easiest and most satisfactory sweet herbs to grow. These small and dainty onions are hardy perennials that can be propagated from seed but are commonly and more easily propagated from the matted clumps of tiny bulbs from which sprout the tops so prized by the cook. At any time of the year when the ground is not frozen, set out two clumps. The more you cut the grassy leaves, the more tender the new shoots are. Cut until freezing weather turns the tops brown.

All summer long, fresh green sprouts come and come again, and at the same time the old clumps enlarge until very soon you will have sufficient increase to warrant dividing. Dig a clump of chives, pull it apart four ways, and you will have four plants which are actually four clumps of many little onions. Set them 8 inches apart and let blossom those you do not need for the salad bowl or cooking. The leaves will grow in sprays about a foot tall and the ornamental flowers will top the leaves with soft tufts of light purple blossoms that are an addition to any flower garden. A border of chives is very decorative.

Chives do best in rich soil, in full sun. They thrive better with a dressing of good compost or barn manure but will live in less rich soil.

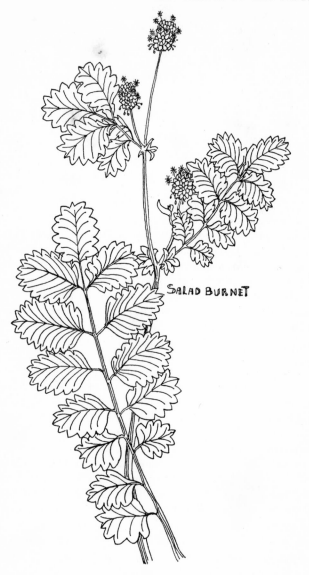

SALAD BURNET

Costmary (*Chrysanthemum Balsamita* var.
   tanacetoides)   HARDY PERENNIAL
Bible Leaf, Alecost, Sweet Mary   SUB-ZERO WINTERS

In colonial days, a leaf of costmary was often used by church-goers to mark the place in the Bible during worship, and so the plant is known as Bible leaf.

Costmary is a tall, long-leafed, decorative salad herb and a great spreader. If given good garden soil and no attention, one plant will suddenly produce a dozen more. New roots grow horizontally underground and send up new stalks.

The blunt, oblong or oval, slightly toothed leaves may grow nearly a foot long. The stems bear rayless yellow flowers at a height of about 5 feet. The whole effect with the light green foliage is pleasing.

Costmary is very hardy and rugged. Old plants can be dug at any time of the year that the ground can be worked, and it is a good policy to divide old plants to keep the growth from becoming weedy. Pull the roots apart and replant at intervals of a foot.

Costmary will thrive in good soil, in sun or semi-shade. In the small garden, we advise confining it with a metal plate (see diagram).

                                                  HARDY BIENNIAL
Cress, Upland (*Barbarea praecox*)   ZERO WINTERS

Upland cress—not to be confused with peppergrass (*Lepedium sativum*) a smallish plant with lacy leaves and a very strong pepper flavor—has leaves that look like those of water cress, only much larger. Upland cress can be used either for flavor or as a salad by itself.

Seeds of this member of the mustard family germinate readily when sown in early spring. You need not thin the seedlings and the more you cut the low mat of leaves, the faster the new and tender leaves grow. Old leaves are tough.

Upland cress is edible until freezing weather comes when the leaves wilt. In a cold climate, however, cress lives over the winter with a covering of salt hay. The leaves may be used for a fresh salad in spring until the plants blossom and make seed, which they do shortly.

	HARDY ANNUAL
Dill (*Anethum graveolens*)	SELF-SOWS
1 package of seeds	TEMPERATE ZONE

Dill is a pretty, annual sweet herb with smooth, bluish-green round stems bearing a lacy, feathery growth of blue-green leaves and delicate umbrella-like clusters of small yellow flowers. The stalks often grow 3 feet tall.

The seeds were formerly called Meeting House seeds because they were taken to church to munch during the long services.

Dill is easily wind-whipped and knocked to the ground. When planting, sow thickly and do not thin. Let the spindly stalks lean upon one another for support.

Dill dies soon after setting seed or with the frost.

Garlic (*Allium sativum*)	HARDY PERENNIAL
1 or 2 bulbs	SUB-ZERO WINTERS

Garlic, a member of the lily family, needs rich organic soil to have a normal growth. Plant in the fall, or the very early spring. One or two bulbs will probably raise all the garlic you will use. Do not set the whole bulb in the ground. A garlic bulb is composed of cloves, each of which will produce a plant. Separate the bulb in your hands and set the cloves 4 inches apart in a trench about an inch deep. Cover with loose soil. The rather uninteresting plants grow about 18 inches high with narrow green leaves.

Lovage (*Levisticum officinale*)	
Smallage, Smellage	HARDY PERENNIAL
2 plants (or 1 package of seeds)	SUB-ZERO WINTERS

Lovage, a sweet herb, is a handsome, herbaceous perennial. Some of the old plants at Hemlock Hill are over 6 feet tall. The round hollow stems, the large shining celery-like leaves, the rather inconspicuous yellow flower umbels combine to make a

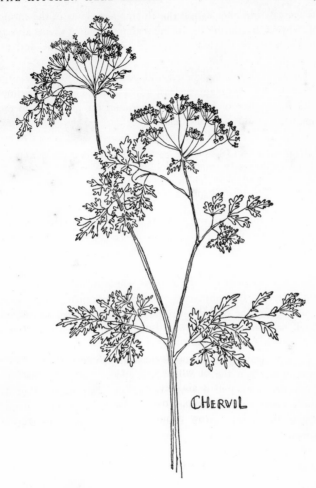

CHERVIL

rugged plant that is easy to grow. It may be propagated from
seed sown in early spring but the seedlings grow slowly and,
for use the first season, it is wiser to buy plants. Old beds may

be increased by root division of the mother plants in the spring of the year, for during the spring season, succulent shoots appear on the sides of the main root and may be cut away and replanted.

Lovage requires a rich soil and good organic fertilizer; sun or semi-shade. Set plants at least a foot apart. The leaves yellow with the coming of freezing weather, and the plant dies to the ground.

Marjoram, Sweet (*Majorana hortensis*)   TENDER PERENNIAL
1 package of seeds

This small Mediterranean sweet herb was formerly classified botanically as an *Origanum,* and is sometimes incorrectly identified with the Italian oregano. Its manner of growth, however, as well as the flavor distinguishes it. Today it is classified not as an *Origanum* but separately, as *Majorana hortensis.*

Sweet marjoram is a perennial in warm climates but must be treated as an annual in the regions where the winter temperatures are low. It is unnecessary to keep these plants in a greenhouse during the cold months in the northern states because an excellent crop may be obtained each year from seed sown early in the spring, as soon as the ground can be worked. The tiny seeds germinate well, although they take about three weeks to come up. When the seedlings first appear, one is inclined to think that they will amount to nothing, but allow about as much space for them as for parsley. After danger of cutworm is past, thin marjoram to about 5 inches, because one day the plants will seem to shoot upward. Soon thereafter each small bush is about a foot to 15 inches high, with a mass of soft, small, gray-green pungent leaves. Before fall, the gardener may make two cuttings. The flowers are small, white, and inconspicuous, with green bracts.

There is another marjoram called pot marjoram, which has a good flavor (see *Origanum*).

Mint (*Mentha spicata*)
Spearmint   HARDY PERENNIAL
2 plants   SUB-ZERO WINTERS

This sweet herb, used in mint julep and lamb sauce, is fussy about its environment, but when satisfied, is a rampant spreader. It needs water but will not grow in boggy land unless the bog is drained. If you wish to plant a large bed, select a spot where there is a drip from a rain spout, splashings from a bird bath, or where water washes off a road during rainstorms, or some similar spot where dampness lingers but does not make long-lasting mud.

Mint thrives in full sun but will endure semi-shade, if other conditions are to its liking. It needs rich soil and if it is grown in a bed by itself, keep the soil from pH 5.2 to pH 6.7. This is the range of acidity and alkalinity recommended by the big commercial growers, on organic soils.

Spearmint can be propagated from seed but is usually started from underground stolons. Watch the growth of spearmint and you will soon know what a stolon is. The plant sends out vigorous purplish horizontal stems that lengthen until each tip touches soft earth, then the stem goes down, 'head first' under the soil. Presently, this buried horizontal stem sends up a new stem from its tip. A new plant can be detached by cutting with a spade or sharp trowel in the space between the new and old stems. If you have an old bed, it is well to use a spade during the spring season and chop the earth at intervals of a foot. This will separate the plants and will give new vigor to the plants. Mint dies to the ground with frost, and does not sprout again in cold climates until late spring. The early growth is often more horizontal than upright, with the plants low and bushy, but when the hot days come, the square stems grow upward, tall and straight to a height of 2 or 3 feet. The blossoms are whorls of inconspicuous pale purple flowers on spikes.

SWEET CICELY

Nasturtiums (*Tropaeolum minus*)
1 package of seeds   TENDER ANNUAL

Be sure to buy the dwarf nasturtiums. Even the dwarf tends
to grow too high for a low border, and only a very few seeds
are necessary for the two short rows. Thin to 6 inches and leave
at least 10 inches' space between the last seed and the rosemary
plants (see diagram).

Plant the seeds in a little trench about ¾ inch deep after all
danger of frost is over, for nasturtiums are sensitive to frost.
The pretty flowers are too well known to need description here,
but not so well known are the uses of the plant as a sweet and
salad herb.

Origanum (English variety: *Origanum*
  vulgare)   HARDY PERENNIAL
Wild Marjoram   SUB-ZERO WINTERS

Origanum—'delight of the mountains' to the Greeks—is commonly called wild marjoram, but we call this sweet herb by the
botanical name of the genus to which it belongs, *Origanum*, to
avoid confusion with sweet marjoram and pot marjoram (see
marjoram). The uncertainty that exists among herb growers
over the several species of *Origanum* and their nomenclature is
further confused by the product sold in Italian stores under the
name oregano. Evidently it is any species of marjoram that
happens to flourish in the region in Italy where the product is
packaged.

The origanum, or wild marjoram, that grows in America is
of inferior flavor, a rank spreader, and should not be given
garden space, but the origanum, or wild marjoram that grows
in England, is a different strain, and bears a fine pungent leaf.
The English variety has a characteristic way of growing, with
the roots horizontal and the stems straight up at almost right
angles to a height of 20 inches or more, at which height the
pinkish flowers bloom.

English origanum may be propagated from seeds but seeds
are hard to obtain in America. The plants themselves are more

often sold. Each plant needs about a square foot or more for spreading, and established plants are easily propagated in spring by layering or root division.

Of the several species of *Origanum* interesting to the herb grower, Dittany of Crete excites the imagination. The wooly-leafed, white-flowered Dittany is not hardy in cold climates.

Parsley (*Petroselinum hortense*)   HARDY BIENNIAL
1 package of seeds   SUB-ZERO WINTERS

There are usually three kinds of garden parsley offered in seed catalogues: the plain, the curly leafed, and the root parsley. We are concerned here only with the first two. The choice between the plain and curly leafed is entirely yours.

The curly leafed is a prettier garnish and it dries a greener color than the plain and has as good flavor. Both do equally well in rich soil but, to the novice, it often seems that parsley has no intention of coming up at all. It is said that this sweet herb has to go nine times to the devil and back before it will sprout. Certainly it is slow to germinate but can be hastened by soaking the seeds in water overnight. Thin the seedlings to about 4 inches.

Parsley has a long season. It can be planted at the same time as the peas in spring; neither frost nor the first freezing weather of fall affect it, and even when the temperature drops near the zero point, the leaves stay green. In very cold weather, however, the leaves lose their flavor.

A crop planted in mid-summer will produce fresh leaves for kitchen use the following spring and will continue to grow until the flower stalks appear, when the plants go to seed. The inflorescence of parsley is quite decorative, the yellowish green flowers borne in compound umbels on stalks about 30 inches high.

CHIVES

Pennyroyal, English (*Mentha Pulegium*)
Pudding Grass   HARDY PERENNIAL
1 plant   ZERO WINTERS

This true mint does not grow erect like spearmint. The stems of English pennyroyal are prostrate, about 20 inches long, and the leaves with their characteristic cool minty fragrance are small and oval, no more than a half inch in length and softly hairy. The flowers are small, bluish-lilac, in axillary whorls.

English pennyroyal can be set out when the frost-resistant plants such as peas and lettuce are planted, and new pennyroyal plants may be obtained by root division in the spring. This sweet herb is no spreader like its cousin spearmint, and need not be confined.

Cover English pennyroyal with salt hay when the ground freezes, in sub-zero climates.

Rosemary (*Rosmarinus officinalis*)
2 plants   TENDER PERENNIAL

Rosmarinus is Latin meaning 'sea-dew,' an apt name for this evergreen shrub, indigenous to the Mediterranean coast of France and to the neighboring chalk hills. The green succulent leaves are gray on the underside and somewhat similar in form to those of yew but longer, not shiny, and very strongly, res-inously aromatic. The light blue racemes of flowers are attractive to bees.

In cold climates before freezing weather comes, rosemary plants must be brought into the house in pots, or wintered in a cold green house, or heeled-in deep in a cold frame.

The ornamental shrubs will grow up to 4 feet high but take several years to reach this height and so will remain small enough for the space allotted on our diagram, for quite some time.

This sweet herb may be propagated from seed, but the seeds are slow to germinate, and the small seedlings grow slowly. Start with plants and propagate rosemary by layering or cuttings.

As may be inferred from its native habitat, rosemary needs lime. A few eggshells or wood ashes dug in around the shrubs will supply the extra lime needed.

Sage, Garden (*Salvia officinalis*)
2 plants

HARDY PERENNIAL
SUB-ZERO WINTERS

Softly gray-green, garden sage is pungent in aroma and flavor, a very ornamental subshrub. This native of the Mediterranean region grows 1½ to 2 feet tall. The downy, pebbly leaves are 2½ to 3½ inches long, narrow oblong in shape; the flowers are purple, the new stems soft, the old stems hard and woody. Cut well back in summer during harvest, allowing time for a good new growth before winter. The leaves of sage stay green almost all winter in cold northern climates; in spring most old leaves die and fall. As soon as the plant gives evidence of vigor and new young leaves appear, cut it back to within about 6 inches of the ground to allow a completely soft stem growth for the first harvest.

This sweet herb is easily raised from seed but the seedlings are too small for cutting the first season. It is advisable, therefore, to start your sage bed with year-old plants. Set plants 1 foot apart. Established plants can be used for propagation by cuttings or by layering branches, or, in the case of very old plants, root division. When sage plants are 5 or 6 years old, they usually have a wide and very woody growth at ground level. These old plants quite often die in winter. At this time, plants are best renewed, which may be done quite easily by root division. In the spring, dig old plants and salvage all the best growth by ripping off heels of the strongest, most vital looking stems, making sure there are roots attached. Plant these root divisions, and discard the hard, woody core of the mother plant.

There is a white-flowered variety of garden sage that is very decorative. There is also an excellent variety known as Holt's Mammoth, which does not set seed. It is of course necessary to buy plants to start a bed of Holt's Mammoth.

COSTMARY

Savory, Summer (*Satureia hortensis*)   ANNUAL
1 package of seeds   FROST-FREE MONTHS ONLY

This European annual is easily propagated from seed. In
northern climates it should be sown the week before Decoration
Day. Summer savory cannot withstand frost.

The plants are erect, about 18 inches in height, and branch
out quite far. They are best grown fairly thick because they are
spindly and easily knocked to the ground with wind or rain.
Thin to not more than 4 inches apart.

The leaves of this sweet herb are small, narrow, long, and
downy, and the small, pale flowers are usually purplish, sometimes pinkish or white, giving the plants a gossamer appearance.

Shallots (*Allium ascalonicum*)
About a half dozen bulbs   HARDY PERENNIAL

This small onion from Syria is an easily grown potherb. The
bulbs are composed of cloves, somewhat larger and less numerous than those of garlic. Separate each bulb and plant the
cloves about 4 inches apart in an inch-deep trench, early in the
spring. The hollow leaves are much like those of a common
onion only more numerous, narrower, and shorter and soon fall
prostrate on the ground. The flowering stem is erect, about 22
inches high. The bulbs are a pinkish-white color.

Tarragon (*Artemisia Dracunculus*)
Estragon   HARDY PERENNIAL
4 plants   SUB-ZERO WINTERS

Tarragon is an herbaceous perennial and dies to the ground
in the fall. During summer the erect branching plants grow
about 2 feet high and if the small smooth narrow leaves are not
cut at this height, the stem will bear very small, round, inconspicuous whitish-green flowers which rarely set seed.

If you find tarragon seeds for sale, do not buy them, for they
will not be the true or, as it is commonly called, French tarragon.
Chances are you will be getting Russian tarragon which can be

raised from seed, and it is an annual of inferior flavor. There are other tarragons, none of culinary value.

Estragon, as the true tarragon is called in France, must be propagated from cuttings or by division of roots in the spring. The latter is the easier and more satisfactory method. All plants that are 4 or 5 years old should be divided. Plants of true tarragon may be bought at almost any large nursery. Set them about a foot apart in a well-drained location. Good drainage is especially necessary for tarragon; in sub-zero climate, it is a good practice to cover your plants during the winter because an open winter may mean loss of immature tarragon subjected to heaving of soil during January thaws.

Thyme, Garden (*Thymus vulgaris*)   HARDY PERENNIAL
6 plants   SUB-ZERO WINTERS

Garden or common thyme is easily grown from seed but because the seedlings will not be large enough for use the first season, it is advisable to buy plants the first year. Set them about 15 inches apart. Old plants can be propagated by root division, and division is advisable after three years because old plants tend to become woody.

This ancient sweet herb of the Mediterranean region makes a pretty edging plant. The stems are usually decumbent near the center of the plant, erect around the margin which makes for low-growing shrubby plants about 11 inches tall, with small deep green leaves and pretty small lilac flowers.

Thyme is hardy in cold northern climates but during open winters it will make a quicker fresh growth in spring if it is given some winter cover.

For Carpeting Thyme for paths and terraces see Chapter 7. Notes on growing other culinary herbs are given in Chapter 6.

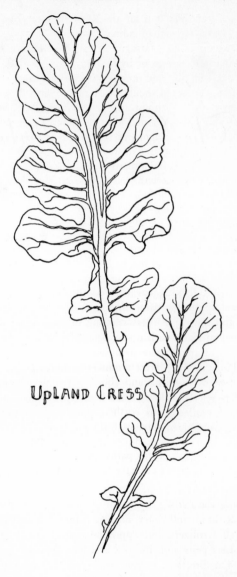

UpLAND CRESS

2

The Growing Herbs

'Gentlewomen, if the ground be not too wet, may doe themselves much good by kneeling upon a Cushion and weeding. And thus both sexes might divert themselves from Idleness, and evill Company, which oftentimes prove the ruine of many ingenious people.'

William Coles, 1657.

THE GARDENER has enjoyed the 'smell of Earth new turned up'; he has planned, fertilized, limed, deep dug, and planted, and now anticipates walking in the garden to pick a lemon-flavored leaf, another that tastes like cucumbers, another of the flavor of anise; still others pungent and strange or hot as pepper. He will find himself, however, looking at a stunted growth of herbs and a lusty crop of weeds unless he maintains the garden scientifically. A well-kept, thrifty looking, sweet scented herb garden is the result of good garden practice, and once again we wish to emphasize the point that successful herb growers do not emulate the husbandry of the all but abandoned farm. Yet very little work is required for the maintenance of the garden shown in the diagram in the end paper, provided that the necessary tasks are done on time. The most important points for keeping the herbs growing are taken up in the following order: cultivation and water; organic plant foods best for herbs; commercial fertilizers, lime, and soil tests; methods of propagation; insect pests and diseases; and winter protection in cold climates. The directions are specifically for the garden of twenty-four basic culinary herbs listed in Chapter 1, but in general apply to most herbs and smaller or larger gardens.

Cultivation and Water

Cultivation in an herb garden is necessary not only to kill weeds but also to prevent runoff of the beneficial rain. It also creates a dry mulch on the soil's surface so that moisture is stored. Unlike plowing—or spading, its equivalent in a small garden—which should be deep, cultivation should be shallow in order to prevent injury to roots near the surface. In a small garden, therefore, use the hoe or hand cultivator frequently, but make each stroke shallow. Like most garden plants, culinary herbs do poorly in dry weather, and when rainfall is scant, sprinkle the herb plants in the evening with the garden hose, and do it thoroughly, wetting the soil down to a depth of about three inches. Merely settling the dust will do more harm than good.

Cow Manure

There is no question but that well-rotted cow manure is un-surpassed as a fertilizer for herbs. It adds humus, which improves the structure of the soil, is one of the best sources of nitrogen, and also supplies some phosphorus and potash and other nutrients. As to the amount of cow manure most beneficial for the small kitchen herb garden (12' x 14'), it is safe to top dress with 4 bushels in spring or fall. One internationally recognized English authority * on herbs recommends applying several times that amount of manure in spring, or a bushel to a square yard, but the amount will of course depend upon condition of the soil in a particular region, and also on the availability of manure. Today, in many sections of the country, cow manure is hard to obtain and most farmers who do sell it, ask an exorbitant price for a cubic yard.

However, commercial dried cow manure is available in most feed stores and garden shops. This dried organic matter is handier for the small-time gardener to use than regular cow

* M. Grieve, *Culinary Herbs and Condiments*. Harcourt, Brace and Company, 1934, p. 13.

DILL

manure because it is in a concentrated form and sold in quantities to suit his needs, and, of great importance, packaged neatly
in bags that can be stored in a tool shed or a garage. Small
amounts can be dug in around the perennial plants with a
trowel as required. The dried cow manure is not only less messy
to use but free of noxious weeds and insect eggs that are often
found in fresh manure. Apply about 18 pounds to a 12- by 14-
foot area in the spring.

Compost

In the days when the family cow and horse were as common
as the family dog and cat, there was no need to debate which
organic matter was best for the home garden. Today the compost heap takes the place of the manure pile. Like barn manure,
compost is a good source of nitrogen, supplies some phosphorus,
potash, and other nutrients needed in the herb garden, as well as
improving the structure of the soil. Also it has the distinct
advantage of being produced at the cost of only a little work.
Compost is made from any non-woody vegetation such as leaves,
so often burned during the fall clean-up, lawn clippings, potato
peelings, carrot tops, plus any vegetable matter that normally
accumulates on a place, with the exception of noxious weeds in
the seed stage and plants that show signs of disease. If there is
mildew on the pea vines or any unhealthy appearance to the
residue of plants, burn them rather than add to the compost
pile. Kitchen garbage, including meat scraps, can be composted
but will attract mice and rats. A shallow natural pit is a good
place for a compost pile, if available, and an artificial 'pit'
(4' x 5') is easily built of cinder blocks, about four blocks high.

There are two ways to build a compost pile: one, the natural
or organic method, and the other, with chemicals that hasten
decomposition. To follow the organic method, alternate layers
of vegetation, about six inches thick, with a few shovelsful of
garden soil, which provides desirable bacteria; turn the pile
occasionally with a fork; and water regularly but do not drench
because too much water will leach away the nutrients. This
natural organic compost will take at least eighteen months
before it is sufficiently rotted to use. Decomposition can be

hastened so that it is possible to use one summer's compost the following spring by the addition of agricultural (hydrated) lime at the rate of a half a pound to each layer. Wood ashes are an excellent source of potash and contain a little lime, and every shovelful from the fireplace, stove, or brush pile should be salvaged, if not for the compost pile, then for direct application on the garden. Culinary herbs respond particularly well to wood ashes. About three-quarters of a pound of superphosphate, or a commercial fertilizer high in nitrogen, sprinkled between the layers of vegetation and soil in the compost pile will also hasten decomposition, but this is not essential.

Add compost to the herb garden at the same rate as cow manure.

Hen Manure

Hen manure is often inexpensive today, or sometimes even available for the labor of cleaning the hen houses of a chicken farmer who does not raise his own chicken feed and has no use for the droppings. If you can obtain hen manure at low cost, take a load and compost it, but do not use it fresh on the herb garden, for unrotted hen manure will burn the plants. In any case, use less of it than cow manure because it contains almost twice as much nitrogen. It is an excellent source of phosphorus, containing over five times as much of that important element as does cow manure, and therefore is good for soils with a phosphorus deficiency. There is no appreciable difference in the amount of potash contained in the two manures. Horse, sheep, and steer manure all have more nitrogen than cow, but hen manure has the most.

Peat Moss

Should the gardener be fortunate enough to have a bog on the farm, he will have a source of natural organic fertilizer in the form of muck, or peat moss. Native peat is good humus and a natural source of nitrogen, phosphorus, and potash, although it contains less of these elements than is found in barn manure. If, however, peat is available at no cost except for the haulage, it makes cheap fertilizer. Peat moss can, of course, be

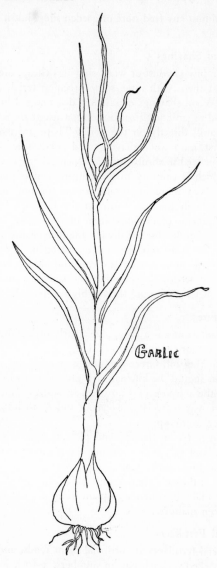

GARLIC

bought in almost any feed store or garden shop, but it is usually expensive.

Sawdust and Shavings

If you can buy sawdust or wood shavings cheap, order a load and compost them with lime, some green material, and some phosphate. Wood shavings or sawdust decomposed in this way make a good organic fertilizer but do not use these by-products from a sawmill directly on the herbs. There are two reasons for this: First, most wood shavings and sawdust are somewhat acid and beneficial to shrubs such as blueberries that require an acid soil which is contrary to the requirement of most herbs. Second, an even more important reason for not using these wood products in the raw form on the herb garden is that during the process of decomposition of the wood, the micro-organisms responsible for the decay—the beneficial bacteria that help make compost—rob the soil of nitrogen. They do this because they require nitrogen and can find almost none in the undecomposed wood. Be sure that the shavings and sawdust used on the herb garden are thoroughly composted.

Green Manure

Green manure means a crop, particularly of legumes or winter rye, grown for the purpose of adding organic matter in the raw form to the soil. Green manure is not for the small-time gardener but should the kitchen herb grower want to condition a field for the purpose of future expansion, green manure is the cheapest way to reclaim worn-out soil or to improve land that has been over-cropped.

Plant winter rye in the fall and plow it under deep in the spring. On land that is idle during the summer months, sow one of the legumes such as soy beans, sweet clover, alfalfa, and plow under in the fall. Legumes are able to take nitrogen from the air and make it available to plants, and are the most beneficial of green manures.

Commercial Fertilizers

Commercial fertilizers are artificial plant foods, and the contents are marked on each bag in numbers. 5–10–5 is the fertilizer for general garden use and the numbers mean that there are 5 pounds of nitrogen (N), 10 pounds phosphoric acid (P_2O_5), and 5 pounds potash (K_2O) in every 100 pound bag. The order is always the same; first nitrogen, then phosphoric acid, and then potash, alphabetical order and easy to remember.

These three are the principal plant foods in which soils are most frequently deficient. If you find, by testing, a deficiency of one of these elements, commercial fertilizer will help decrease the deficiency more quickly than will the organics because in the chemical (commercial) form, nitrogen and other elements are released and made available more quickly to the plants. Commercial fertilizers, however, should always be used sparingly. Too much will burn plants, and in a small garden, a mere tablespoonful to each plant applied a few inches from the main stem is sufficient.

In addition to the general garden fertilizer, there are other commercial fertilizers on the market, some with only one nutrient.

Lime

Because most herbs do best in a slightly alkaline soil, acid soil should be limed. For the small kitchen herb garden, a little lime may be salvaged from the refuse can in the form of eggshells, and dug in around the roots of the plants. Wood ashes contain a little lime, but if you lack these, use commercial lime. For the small garden, buy agricultural (hydrated) lime because it is quick acting and in a form more readily available to plants than is ground limestone. In areas where the soil is not naturally alkaline, it is a fairly safe practice to add about 2 pounds of lime a year to a 12 foot by 14 foot space. Sprinkle it on the garden, preferably in the fall, making sure to keep it about five inches from the perennials to prevent burning of the crowns.

For the herbalist who grows herbs in large quantities, it is more economical to use ground limestone which is cheaper but must be spread a long time before planting. It takes three or four months to react with the soil and so must be applied in the fall to be available to plants by springtime.

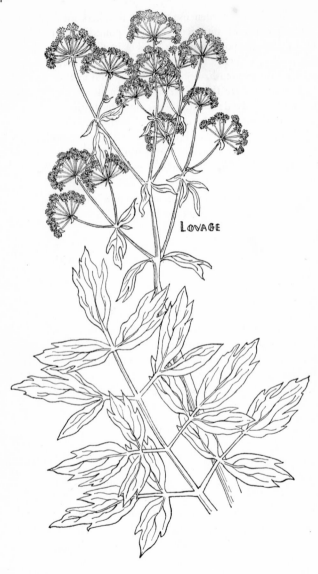

LOVAGE

Soil Tests

In addition to nitrogen, phosphorus, potash, and lime, for good plant nutrition there also must be small amounts of iron, magnesium, sulphur; and very small amounts of the so-called trace elements, manganese, boron, chlorine, iodine, zinc, and copper. Chances are that if you use organic fertilizer regularly and lime as needed, there will be enough nitrogen, phosphorus, potash, and these other elements in your soil. A deficiency, or sometimes an overabundance, of any one element, however, can mean failure of herb crops. Failure due to overabundant supply or to a deficiency can be guessed at by the appearance of the plants, by color other than green in the leaves, by stunted growth, and so on, but can be analyzed properly only by a soil test. The modern way to farm, even for the small kitchen gardener, is to send a soil sample each year to a laboratory qualified to make the test.

A soil test tells whether a garden lacks humus; it gives specific quantities of fertilizer to add, either organic or commercial, and it gauges to an exact degree the amount of lime to apply, in terms of the soil's pH. pH is a symbol used by horticulturists to denote the degree of acidity or alkalinity of a soil. A pH of less than 7 is on the acid side, over 7 is alkaline. Few plants will grow in a soil testing 'below pH 3.5 or above pH 9.0. The most favorable pH range for most crop plants is 6.2–7.2.' * Herbs will grow within a range of 6.2–7.2, but the best pH for the kitchen herb garden is 7.0–7.2.

Anyone desiring information concerning soil testing in his own state should write directly to the College of Agriculture of the land-grant college located in the respective state. The tests are done either by experiment stations or by extension service, and in some instances, facilities are provided for making these tests in the counties. In many states, a nominal fee is charged for running the tests, in some states, there is no charge.

* *Hunger Signs in Crops* (a symposium). The American Society of Agronomy and the National Fertilizer Association, 1949.

Propagation of Perennial Herbs

There are three methods of propagating perennial herbs whereby a grower may both have his plant and sell it. These are root division, layering, and cuttings. The method most successful with each herb is noted under specific growing instructions for each plant.

Root division means simply that one plant is divided into two or more. Many herbs are easily reproduced this way, and for a few such as tarragon, which does not set seed, it is the best method. To divide tarragon, select a large plant, at least 2, and preferably 3 or 4 years old, and cut back the stems to within about 4 inches of the ground. Then dig the plant with a fork, grasp the roots in both hands and pull. You will find that many of the roots, though intertwined, are quite independent of each other and separate easily, particularly in the spring, which is the season for propagation in cold northern climates. In the fall a newly divided plant may not make sufficient growth to winter over. Plant each division and water regularly until it is established.

Some herbs, such as thyme and sage, become woody the third season, and in order to divide them, it is sometimes necessary to cut away old growth with a hatchet, but the less cutting the better. In this type of plant, it is a good practice to select a stem, or a section of the old plant where the growth is soft, and rip off a 'heel' with small roots attached. Discard the center woody core.

The second and easiest way to propagate many herbs is by layering. Origanum, thyme, and sage, and some others layer themselves. To induce layering, peg down a stem of a mature and vigorous plant in soft earth, then cover pegged section with soil, and water daily. Wire coat hangers, cut in short pieces and bent to form staples, make satisfactory 'pegs.' When there is a good root growth on the buried stem, cut the connection with the mother plant. Like root division, layering is most successful in the spring when plants are making a quick new growth.

The third and best-known method of propagation is by cut-

SWEET MARJORAM

tings, commonly called 'slips.' Cuttings also do best in the spring. Some herbs, such as rosemary, will make roots if kept in a glass of water, but for the most part it is better to use a flat, half filled with clean sand or, better still, vermiculite, which is sterile. The other necessary equipment is a sharp knife. To take a 'slip,' make a right-angle cut in a stem just below a node. This exposes a flat surface which will have a direct contact with the sand or other material in which the stem is set. Also, a right-angle cut places the exposed surface evenly below a node, whereas a slanting cut brings the knife too near the node on one side, and on the other too far below.

Snip off all but a few top leaves on a cutting, then set it immediately. In general, it is not a good practice to let cuttings lie in wet paper before planting, as some people recommend. The time is too short to heal the cut, and no good purpose is accomplished except with very succulent, soft growth like geraniums, which, if allowed to remain in wet paper unplanted for twenty-four hours, will not heal but will shrink, and when set and watered, the subsequent swelling of the 'slip' will completely fill the hole made for planting.

To set a cutting properly, make a hole in the propagating material, and place the cutting in this hole, tamping gently around the stem until the hole is filled. Water. Then place the flat in a cold frame but cover the glass with newspapers most of the day or the hot sun will wither the cuttings. The most important factor in rooting cuttings is to water regularly and always keep the 'ground' damp, but not drenched. When the cuttings have good roots, which for most will take at least six weeks, set them in pots filled with good potting soil, and place the pots where they may be watched and watered until the roots are established, or set the cuttings directly in the garden in a shady spot.

Hormone powders undoubtedly hasten root growth on cuttings. Many people have found, however, that while hormone treated cuttings do get off to a faster start, they are overtaken by those untreated which start slowly but keep growing more steadily.

INSECTICIDES

Contrary to popular belief, herbs are subject to insect pests and disease, at least as much as vegetables and garden flowers. But there is a special problem connected with fighting pests in the herb garden. Because many culinary herbs are grown for their leaves, it is unwise ever to spray or dust them with poisonous or toxic preparations. The herb grower should use no insecticides such as Paris Green, Bordeaux Mixture, or D.D.T. in any part of the growing area. Fortunately the pests and diseases most commonly encountered in the herb garden can be controlled by one of three non-poisonous insecticides discussed below, with the occasional use of other insecticides in small selected areas adjoining the herb garden, combined with hand picking.

'Hand picking of the larger beetles, caterpillars and plant bugs,' says the United States Department of Agriculture in the Bulletin on the insects and diseases of vegetable gardens, 'will often give satisfactory control in a small garden and eliminate the need for applying insecticides.' *

Incidentally this bulletin has pictures of pests common in the vegetable garden, some of which attack herbs. The practices recommended may be applied by the herb grower, except those involving use of poisonous sprays or dusts.

When the gardener finds it necessary to use insecticides, he will have to spray less often if he anticipates the insect pests and diseases that he knows will appear in his area each year. Insecticides are best applied in the cool of evening. When sprayed in the hot sun, or when the temperature is high, the leaves of certain plants will wilt and curl. Dust should be applied either early in the morning or in the late afternoon so that the night's dew will make the dust adhere to the leaves.

* *Vegetable Gardeners' Handbook on Insects and Diseases,* Miscellaneous Publication No. 605, United States Department of Agriculture. Price 20 cents.

Spearmint

For the Herb Garden

Rotenone

   Dust: a 75% rotenone powder (prepared)
   Spray: a 75% rotenone powder (prepared)—3 tablespoons
      mixed in a gallon of water.

Pyrethrum

   Dust (prepared)
   Spray: a prepared spray material mixed with water according
      to directions on package.

Sulphur

   Dust (prepared)
   Spray: mix a 95% wettable powder at the rate of ⅛ pound
      to 2½ gallons of water.

In Areas Outside the Herb Garden

D.D.T.

   D.D.T. is a toxic spray and should never be used in the
culinary herb garden. When, however, certain insect pests that
are not killed by rotenone or pyrethrum come in numbers that
defy hand picking, it is a good practice to spray surrounding
areas with this or a similar insecticide to give some measure
of control. Use D.D.T. only when absolutely necessary in small,
strategic locations where the pests are found in greatest numbers.
D.D.T. has a residual effect that lasts for many weeks.

   The spray is made from a 50% wettable powder, mixed at
the rate of 2 level tablespoons to a gallon of water. Be sure to
buy agricultural D.D.T., because the household preparation
contains a petroleum product harmful to plants.

Marlate

   Marlate is a 50% methoxychlor insecticide, believed to be
non-toxic to warm-blooded animals and birds, and can therefore
be used a little more freely than D.D.T. to fight the same insects. Like D.D.T. it is effective when used in selected areas
outside the herb garden, combined with hand picking in the
garden proper. Should you use marlate on edible leaf plants, be

sure to wash all leaves thoroughly before preparing for the table.

For spray, mix 5 tablespoons marlate to 1 gallon of water and use after every rain. Unlike D.D.T., it has no lasting residual effect.

PESTS AND DISEASES

There follows a list of some of the major insect and other pests and diseases that attack herb plants, with recommended treatment.

Japanese Beetles (*Popillia japonica*)

Among the kitchen herbs that the voracious Japanese beetles attack are lemon balm, basil, borage, costmary, and dill. To control these pests, spray with marlate or D.D.T. any roses or hollyhocks outside the herb garden, grape vines before fruiting, beech trees, and particularly any sassafras in the near-by area, and also of great importance, the wild blackberry and raspberry patches. In short, spray non-culinary plants that are especially liked by the beetles and that grow beyond the border of the kitchen garden, and hand pick those beetles that escape the spray.

This is an effective method of Japanese beetle control in a small area, after the beetles have begun to fly. There are several well-known and tried methods of eradicating these insects in the grub stage and to understand and apply the controls, it is necessary to know the beetle life cycle. A graphic description from the egg stage through the metamorphosis from grub to beetle is given in *The Yearbook of Agriculture,* 1952, published by the United States Department of Agriculture.

Of the greatest importance is the fact that the grub stage is usually spent in sod. It is possible, without using toxic insecticides in the growing area, to cut down the number of grubs that mature by treating turf areas with D.D.T. (or chlordane). The treatment is inexpensive and, according to some entomologists, the amount required does not create a serious hazard in poisoning the soil.

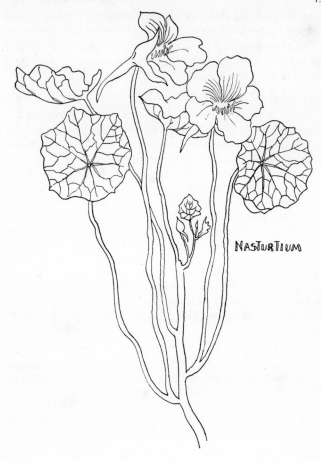

NASTURTIUM

Four-Lined Plant Bug (*Poecilocapus lineatus*)

If the herb grower should observe the tops of dill plants turn-ing brown, with subsequent failure to set seed, he should look for a small but very active winged insect that also attacks roses. This sucking insect can quickly destroy a season's dill crop but is easily controlled with an early application of pyrethrum (dust or spray), repeated if necessary. Once this insect has been recognized in the garden, it is advisable to spray dill and roses before the time of blossoming and thus anticipate the almost certain arrival of the four-lined plant bug.

Larva of the Painted Lady Butterfly (*Vanessa cardui*)

Borage plants, hollyhocks, and some of the artemisias are attacked by a disagreeable looking, blackish, hairy caterpillar that consumes a large amount of vegetation. The larva makes its presence known not only by leaf damage but by the mass of unsightly droppings it deposits on the stems and the mutilated leaves. Its method of attack is to curl up in a leaf, fold the edges like a hammock, and then devour the foliage. Fortunately, the control of this pest is quite easy. With two good applications of rotenone dust the larvae of the painted lady butterfly will usually disappear.

Parsley Worm (*Papilo polyxenes*)

Although it is not an abundant species, few vegetable gardeners are unfamiliar with the gross, fat, green parsley worm with the yellow horns. This striking looking pest has black bands and yellow spots on its green coat. Most people make its acquaintance by the offensive odor it exudes when touched or excited.

This so-called 'worm,' is not a worm in the true sense, but the larva of the beautiful swallow-tail butterfly. It feeds on parsley and other umbelliferous plants including caraway, fennel, and dill. The United States Department of Agriculture recommends control in small gardens by hand picking.

Spittle Insects (*Asphrophora quadrangularis*)

These curious and interesting insects are not always in great enough numbers to harm plants but in some years they develop abundantly, and herbs such as mint become infested with them. They are easily identified by the white froth, the spittle from which the insects make their houses. A spittle insect sucks plants, digests the juice, and churns it out through its alimentary canal with the motion of its tail resembling an egg beater.

When the spittle insects appear on mint or other herbs in any numbers, spray with rotenone or pyrethrum.

Goldenrod Lace Bug (*Corythrica marmorata*)

This small delicate insect, which may be recognized by the white net over the wings, attacks costmary. For control, spray with pyrethrum.

Cutworms

Common cutworms are the larvae of the owlet moth, which lays eggs from early to mid-summer. Not long after, the cutworms hatch and set about feeding on the roots and succulent stems of young plants but at this time the garden is usually well established, the plants tall and strong. The cutworms are small and eat little. It is not until the following spring that much damage is done, at which time the cutworms end their periods of hibernation deep in the earth and come to the surface. Still in the larval stage and soon reaching full size they do great damage among succulent young herbs. They pupate in early or mid-summer and, from that time on, little cutworm damage is done.

A measure of control can be had by protecting the stems of plants with a cardboard or tar paper collar. Use a piece about 3 inches deep and long enough to encircle the stem with about a half an inch of air space around the stem. Set this cardboard guard into the earth, leaving at least one inch above ground.

If you find a place where cutworms are active, evidenced by stems or leaves cut off at the surface, go out early in the morning and dig carefully around the plants. You may often catch several cutworms near the surface at this time of day, but do not look for them later when the sun is high because they go deep in the earth as the temperature rises.

If cutworms are very abundant and more drastic methods are indicated, you may want to try a cutworm bait, a commercial preparation containing toxaphene which is very effective and, according to the entomologist at the Connecticut Agricultural Experiment Station, does not seriously poison the soil or animals

ORIGANUM

or other insects. Also, toxaphene decomposes and thus it does not accumulate.

If you feel, however, as we do, that the fewer chemicals used in the soil, the better the gardening practice, you may prefer to protect large plants when you set them out in the garden, as we suggest above, and plant seeds thickly, allowing a certain percentage for cutworm loss.

Large White Grubs

Large white or pale yellow grubs up to one and a half inches in length are the larvae of the common brown June bug. They are found most often in sod and do great damage by feeding on plant roots. Deep plowing or digging in late autumn will kill many of the hibernating grubs, but there is no real remedy known except to plant thickly and expect a certain amount of loss in newly plowed land.

Snails and Slugs

Snails and slugs do damage to herbs in moist locations, particularly to plants such as woad that have lower leaves hugging the surface of the ground. A little hydrated lime sprinkled around the stems will give some measure of control.

Moles

Moles are *Insectivora,* insect eaters, and their main diet is earthworms and grubs. By extensive tests, in which mice were excluded from the test area, the tulip growers of California found that western moles eat a very small amount of vegetation such as tulip bulbs, wheat, and garden peas, but that the main damage is done by the tunnels the energetic moles make under the roots of plants. The tunnels expose the plant roots which dry out.

Writing in the year 1657, William Coles suggests that 'If you have trouble with Moles in your Garden or other Grounds, put Garlic, Leeks, Onyons in their passages, and they will leap out of the ground immediately.'

For control in the twentieth century there are several kinds of mole traps on the market but a more effective method is to use smoke bombs sold by the Farm Bureau for a few pennies each. Each small cardboard cartridge contains a chemical mixture that ignites when lighted, forming a gaseous smoke that is directed into the mole hole by placing the cartridge in the hole and covering it with earth after touching a match to the fuse.

Another successful method is to drown moles in the spring when the moles are having their young, by placing a garden hose at the entrance to a runway they use regularly. Let the water run until it backs up at the entrance.

In any method of control, it is important to find a runway used every day. To determine the location, press down the raised earth with your foot, and then notice if it is pushed up the following day.

Fungae

Mildew caused by a fungus may be controlled by spraying regularly with sulphur.

Rust

Rust is a common disease of mint. To control, burn infected foliage and spray regularly with sulphur. To assure eradication, start a new bed in a new location with fresh root stock.

Mint Anthracnose—Leopard Spot

Peppermint and wild mint are very susceptible to this disease which is first evidenced by the presence of small brown spots on the leaves and stems. In a small herb garden, start a new bed in a disease-free area with new root stock. In larger gardens, deep plow the old bed so that all foliage, both leaves and stems, are well covered with soil, and, provided that disease-free stolons are planted, there will probably be little or no infection the following spring.

Verticillium Wilt

This most serious mint disease causes stunted growth of plants and they finally yellow and die. The organism that causes wilt persists in the soil and, at the time this book goes to press, the developing of wilt-resistant strains of mint is the method being

PARSLEY

employed to combat the disease. If wilt should strike your mint, contact the nearest agricultural experiment station for latest information on control.

If the insecticides listed in the preceding pages fail to eradicate, or give adequate control of, an unfamiliar sucking or chewing insect, or if you find a leaf withered or spotted for no apparent reason, contact your state Agricultural Experiment Station which you may locate through the local Farm Bureau or state agricultural college. The entomologist in charge will identify any pest unknown to you and recommend the most up-to-date methods of control.

3

The Harvest

'A good House-wife may and will gather store of herbs for the pot, about Lammas, and will dry them and pound them, and in winter they will do good service.'

William Lawson, 1617.

LEAF HERBS TO DRY

Balm, Lemon	Marjoram, Sweet	Rosemary
Basil	Mint	Sage
Chervil	Origanum	Savory, Summer
Chives	Parsley	Tarragon
Lovage	Pennyroyal	Thyme

MATERIALS

Pair of garden shears
Ball of string or
Hardware cloth screen
Mason jars
Canvas or piece of muslin

Small corn mill (F. No. 4) or
rolling pin
Flour sifter
Labels

LEAF HERBS should be harvested when lush green. For the following this means when just coming into bud: basil, chervil, marjoram, mint, lovage, origanum, and summer savory. If you wait for the flowers, many of the leaves will have turned yellow. Two crops may be had each season and all but lovage and origanum may be cut within a few inches of the ground. Leave more foliage on these two herbs, to assure a quick re-

ENGLISH PENNYROYAL

covery and particularly after the second cutting to assure wintering. Tarragon should be harvested as soon as there is a fresh
green growth of about a foot to 14 inches. The plants should
then make enough growth for a second cutting but should be
allowed to go into fall with a fair amount of foliage.

Lemon balm, pennyroyal, thyme, rosemary, and sage can be
gathered at any time there is a full, fresh growth of leaves, and
several crops may be had during the summer, but be sure there
is some new growth to take the plants through the winter.
Plants trimmed to the ground in late summer may winterkill.

Parsley may be harvested as often as it makes a good, healthy
growth, and a late planting will winter over and give a spring
crop. Chives should be cut before there are any yellow leaves.
As soon as the leaves begin to fade, cut to the ground and wait
for a new crop.

When an herb is ready for drying, cut the stems after the
dew is off the grass. This is the accepted way which may have
the virtue of helping to seal the essential oils in the leaves. Para-
doxically, they must be made wet again, for, after cutting, it is
usually necessary to wash them. After washing, spread the herbs
in the shade to drip until the excess water is gone.

There are two good methods of drying leaf herbs: (1) tie
small bunches of herb with string and hang them; (2) spread
the herbs loosely on a frame stretched with rabbit wire which
goes by the trade name of hardware cloth, a coarse galvanized
screening. A third and commercial method, with oven heat,
produces an inferior product because the artificial heat destroys
the essential oils. For the one exception, chives, see below.

Hanging in bunches or spreading on a screen is equally
effective, providing that the curing is done in a really dry atmosphere. The old-fashioned attic pierced by great stone or brick
chimneys is ideal. On clear days the sun beats down on the
peaked roof and assures a perfect climate, while on a chill rainy
day there is certain to be a fire downstairs, either in the fireplace
or the kitchen stove, with heat rising gently into the attic
through the great chimneys. In the modern flat-roofed house,

the best room is the kitchen, particularly in buildings of cinder or cement blocks, which often harbor dampness. A peaked-roof wooden shed is a good substitute for the attic provided there is a stove in use during long, cold rainy spells.

Chives, the exception to the directions above, must be dried by artificial heat. If dried naturally like other leaf herbs, the succulent 'grass' turns yellow and has an inferior flavor. To dry chives properly, spread them thinly in a large roasting pan, set the pan in a slow oven, and turn the 'greens' from time to time. They will not lose their fresh color, so long as the heat is kept low. When dry, prepare in the same manner as other leaf herbs. The product is of particular value to the person who, during the winter months, lives in a city apartment with no sunny window in which to grow a pot of fresh chives.

Final Preparation for the Cook Pot

Once your leaf herbs are dry enough to crumble when rubbed between your fingers, they should be bottled, not only to keep them free from dust but to preserve their strength. They may be bottled in leaf form but certainly the better way to prepare them for the cook is to pulverize them. This assures a fine, stem-free product, easy to measure and as easy to use as pepper and salt. Only mint or other herbs to be used for tea, and bay leaf should be kept in leaf form.

To pulverize leaf herbs, take them from the ceiling or screen where they have been curing and strip the leaves from the stems, either by hand, or by rubbing them gently against a screen of hardware cloth. Then, because the leaves are prone to absorb the least bit of moisture in the atmosphere, spread them on a clean canvas or piece of muslin in full sun for no longer than five minutes. Long exposure to the sun rays will rob them of their volatile oils and make the product weak in flavor, but brief exposure will prevent mold during storage.

After exposure to sun, set the control screw on the corn mill to a fine grind, and feed the leaves into the hopper. Last, sift the pulverized herbs through a common kitchen flour sifter,

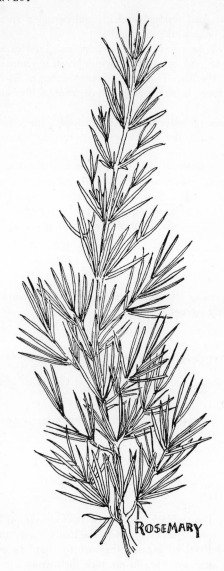

ROSEMARY

discard the small residue of chaff, and bottle in an absolutely dry Mason or any other air-tight jar.

When you have finished pulverizing one kind of herb, take the mill apart and dust it with a clean brush to remove particles clinging to the disc. This will prevent mixing of flavors. After grinding chives, wash the mill, and dry thoroughly before using again.

A fair job of pulverizing can be done with a rolling pin. Prepare the leaves the same way as for grinding, then roll them, sift, and bottle.

Finally, in order to save yourself time in the kitchen, label your products, indicating the date of harvest. A few herbs will retain their aromatic flavor for two years or longer, but most lose their freshness or strength after twelve months.

Those that lose their flavor after one year are:

Balm, Lemon	Parsley
Chervil	Savory, Summer
Chives	Tarragon

The following retain their flavor for longer than a year but not their full strength:

Basil	Mint
Lovage	Origanum
Marjoram, Sweet	Pennyroyal

The following are still aromatic after two years' proper storage:

Rosemary	Thyme
Sage	

SEED HERBS TO HARVEST

Cicely, Sweet	Lovage
Dill	Nasturtiums

The long brown-black seeds of sweet cicely should be picked when ripe, spread out on a tray in the kitchen until thoroughly dry, then pulverized because they are too hard to use whole. When dill seeds are ripe, do not pick them from the plant but cut the stems and hang in bunches in the attic or kitchen for a week or so, then shuck the seeds and spread out on a tray until thoroughly dry. Store in Mason jars. Dill seeds may be used whole or pulverized. Harvest lovage seeds the same way as dill.

The main point to remember with most herb seeds is to harvest only when dead ripe, with the exception of nasturtiums. Nasturtium seeds must be gathered when still soft and immature and pickled at once (see recipes).

Harvesting Bulbs and Roots

Shallots are ready to harvest when the tops lie on the ground. On a dry day, pull the bulbs from the ground, cut off the tops about a half inch from the bulbs, and spread the bulbs outdoors on a rack to dry for at least twenty-four hours. Then store in the coolest corner of the cellar. Like common onions, shallots will not keep near a furnace.

When garlic is mature, the tops wither and turn yellow. Pull the bulbs, braid the tops together in small bunches, and hang in a cool place in the cellar for the winter. Those you do not use in the kitchen should be planted the next season because your own sets produce better bulbs than do those that are not acclimatized to your place.

The directions for harvesting and drying these typical herbs apply to other culinary herbs listed in the book.

Herb Blends

The French *bouquet garni* is a selection of fresh herbs tied in a small bunch and used in soup, stew, and similar dishes. You may make dried *bouquet garni,* using whole dried leaves and tying them together in small squares of cheesecloth but the objection to this method is that the herbs cannot be used in this form for roast meats or other similar recipes. The better method is to bottle blends of dried pulverized herbs which may be added to stews and soups or sprinkled on roasts. Blends are particularly useful to any person, for example, a businesswoman, whose time in the kitchen is limited, because they may be prepared in the few leisure moments she may have. Measure, mix well, and store in labeled jars.

SAGE

Note: In the following blends, one herb in addition to the basic herbs is used, namely celery. If you do not grow celery, dry the leaves of bunches you buy in the store, the same way you do the other leaf herbs.

FOR MEAT LOAF AND MEAT BALLS

4 teaspoons marjoram	¼ teaspoon thyme
2 teaspoons celery	¼ teaspoon lovage
5 teaspoons parsley	

Use 1 level teaspoon to 1 pound of meat.

FOR FISH

4 teaspoons parsley	¼ teaspoon lemon balm
2 teaspoons summer savory	½ teaspoon celery
⅓ teaspoon thyme	1 teaspoon dill, pulverized

Use 1 level teaspoon to 1 pound fish or to 1 pint fish chowder.

FOR SOUPS (Beef stock)

2 teaspoons lovage	1 teaspoon pennyroyal
2 teaspoons parsley	2 teaspoons marjoram or origanum

Use 1 level teaspoon to 1 pint of soup.

FOR SALADS

1 teaspoon basil	¼ teaspoon chives
¼ teaspoon chervil	⅛ teaspoon lovage
¼ teaspoon spearmint	1 teaspoon lemon balm
1 teaspoon tarragon	

Use 1 level teaspoon to a half a cup of vinegar (plain).

FOR POULTRY STUFFING

1½ teaspoons sage	1 teaspoon thyme
1 teaspoon lovage	4 teaspoons parsley
1 teaspoon celery	

Use 1 level teaspoon to 1 cup of stuffing.

Herb Teas

If you should hear two herb lovers talking about such and such a tisane, they are speaking of herb teas. Herb teas are made like ordinary tea, by pouring boiling water over the leaves and letting them steep. The teapot should be of the material good for making regular tea; for example, china or well-glazed pottery, but not metal.

The length of time for steeping and the amount of leaves to use are best determined by personal experience. Start with a few leaves to a cup and steep for two minutes. Too much steeping makes a bitter tea although there are a few medicinal teas that require boiling.

The leaves can be used fresh or dried whole, but not pulverized. The following herbs among the basic twenty-four are well-known tea herbs: lemon balm, mint, pennyroyal, and sage. Spearmint and lemon balm, and spearmint and pennyroyal, are good combinations.

Sage tea was often used in our great grandparents' day for its medicinal value, particularly for colds. Pennyroyal tea is a homely remedy for indigestion. Spearmint used with China or India tea is particularly good iced. Rub the leaves of fresh mint around the top of the pitcher and the room will be permeated with a cooling aroma.

Herbs, other than those mentioned above, sometimes used for tea include: the leaves of bergamot, calamint, catnip, celery, ground ivy, lovage, sweet marjoram, and rosemary; the flowers of chamomile, feverfew, and lavender; the flowers and leaves of tansy.

Herb Vinegars

MATERIALS

A two-quart (or larger) stone or earthenware crock, with cover
Garden shears
Bottles with caps or corks
Glass funnel (or stainless steel)
Wooden spoon
Cheesecloth

SUMMER SAVORY

Filter paper
White wine vinegar, red wine vinegar, or cider vinegar, depending
upon the herbs used.

The following among the basic herbs make good vinegar:
lemon balm, basil, borage, garlic, mint, summer savory, tarragon, and thyme. The recipes call for fresh leaves and are for
vinegars popular today in making French dressing, and pickles,
and for cooking.

TARRAGON OR ESTRAGON VINEGAR

This is the best known and one of the best herb vinegars.
It is made from the tarragon (*Artemisia Dracunculus*), commonly called French, and marketed in France as estragon.

When tarragon is fresh green, gather enough to half fill a
two-quart crock. Cut the stems with the leaves attached, wash
them, and spread on a screen in the shade to drip until dry.
Strip the leaves from main, tough stalks, and cut them up with
kitchen shears. The small, leaf-bearing stems may be used, provided that they are soft and tender, not woody. Bruise the
leaves in the crock with a wooden spoon, then fill the crock
almost to the top with a good grade of full-strength, white wine
vinegar. Let stand for at least three weeks, or until the vinegar
takes on the flavor of the tarragon. Stir every other day with a
wooden spoon.

When the vinegar seems well infused with the essence of
tarragon, remove the leaves and stems from the crock, then filter
the vinegar twice through filter paper, using a glass or stainless
steel funnel. Bottle the vinegar, and before corking place a fresh
sprig of tarragon in each container for decorative effect.

BASIL VINEGAR

Made of the leaves and tender stalks of basil, and with white
wine vinegar, the same way as tarragon.

BURNET VINEGAR

Like tarragon and basil, it is best made with white wine vinegar. Some people use only the leaves, while others also use the

seeds, dried and crushed. The process is the same as for tarragon; the flavor is similar to that of cucumbers.

LEMINT VINEGAR

Made of a combination of fresh mint (spearmint) leaves and
the leaves of lemon balm, infused in cider vinegar. Gather about
3¼ cups of mint leaves, and about ¾ cup of lemon balm leaves
for a two-quart crock. Fill the crock almost to the top with a
good grade of full-strength cider vinegar. Proceed as with tarragon vinegar.

GARLIC VINEGAR

Made with red wine vinegar. Peel and crush enough cloves
of garlic to make a cupful. The cloves may be bruised with a
wooden spoon or put through a coarse grind in the meat grinder.
Place the garlic in a two-quart crock nearly full of the vinegar,
and let infuse for about two weeks, stirring every other day.
Then strain through cheesecloth, filter twice, bottle, and label.

MIXED HERB VINEGAR #1

¾ cup basil leaves   1½ cups chopped chives
¾ cup tarragon leaves   1 bulb garlic

Cut up the basil and tarragon leaves, add the chopped chives,
peel and crush the cloves of one garlic bulb, add the garlic, and
nearly fill a two-quart crock with a good grade of red wine
vinegar. Let infuse for about three weeks, stirring every other
day with a wooden spoon. Strain through cheesecloth, filter
twice, bottle, and label.

MIXED HERB VINEGAR #2

Take ⅕ quart each of:
Chopped chives   Summer savory leaves
Borage leaves   Basil leaves
Lemon balm leaves

Cut up leaves and place with chives in a two-quart stoneware
or earthenware crock. Add two sprigs of thyme, and nearly fill

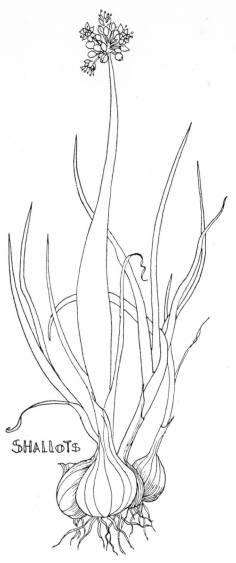

SHALLOTS

the crock with either cider or red wine vinegar. Stir and mash every other day with a wooden spoon. At the end of three weeks strain through cheesecloth, filter twice, bottle, and label.

The vinegar-impregnated leaves of the various herbs, especially tarragon, used in making herb vinegars, can be saved for cooking. Tarragon leaves taste good on fish fillets, and the vinegared leaves of other herbs, a very few at a time, can be added to salads.

4

Herbs in the Kitchen

A pound is a small thing
    When elephants are weighed.
A quart is a mere drop
    When oceans are surveyed.
But may lightning strike,
    And very soon,
The cook who measures herbs
    By tablespoon.

Hemlock Hill Herbal, 1952.

AMATEUR COOKS often make the mistake of using herbs too generously. Herbs should accent and bring out the flavor, not smother the character, of food. Tarragon should complement fish, not disguise the essential fishiness. Unless you are preparing for a very large dinner party, think of herbs in terms of teaspoons, more often half or quarter teaspoons, or a sprinkle, as you use pepper. Better to use too little than too much. The exceptions, where a tablespoon might be used to measure herbs, are noted in the recipes, or in the text under the specific culinary quality of a particular herb.

In general, when more than one herb is called for, each should complement, not disguise, the other. Certain herbs do this naturally. They belong together, while some, unless used with caution, overpower those others used in the same dish.

TARRAGON

FRESH AND DRIED HERBS

Dried herbs are often preferable, even in summer when fresh herbs are available. They blend better than fresh herbs in stews, chowders, and many oven dishes; they are certainly more convenient to use; and they are of special value, because dry measure is exact, to the cook unaccustomed to the strength and flavor of herbs.

Fresh herbs are better in some canapes, herb butters, certain casserole dishes, and especially with shellfish and salads. Shrimps are far fresher tasting when boiled with green dill leaves, although when the garden is snow covered, dill seeds are an acceptable substitute. As for salads, many aspics and certainly all green salads require fresh herbs. Dried herbs should be used in green salads only when neither green herbs nor herb vinegars are available, and, of course, fresh herbs are used for garnish.

The next few pages are devoted to a brief summary of the special culinary quality of the twenty-four basic herbs and is intended as a supplement to the flavor chart.

Lemon Balm

Lemon balm has light green leaves that taste like lemons. It is a good substitute for lemon verbena in a climate where the latter will not winter over. Use it in combination with spearmint to make lemint vinegar, which is good in mint sauce.

Lemon balm is very good with fish, with lamb, and, sparingly, with salads and beef.

Basil

Basil has an affinity with tomatoes. A pinch of dried basil or chopped fresh leaves on sliced tomatoes or in a cup of canned tomato juice improves the flavor of the fruit. Basil is also good in spaghetti sauce, with ham, and in egg dishes, and makes an excellent herb vinegar.

Borage

Borage is a cocktail and salad herb. The ancients believed that this herb would impart courage to anyone who floated a borage

flower in his drink. It will add beauty to the appearance of a
modern cocktail glass and a slight cucumbery flavor to the drink
itself, and it may indeed bring strength of will to the drinker.

One or two very young leaves will impart a slight cucumbery
flavor to a green salad. Old leaves are too tough and hairy to
be eaten.

Burnet, Salad

Salad burnet is, as the name implies, a salad herb. The delicate
young leaves add a pleasant, rather cucumbery flavor to a green
salad and are also used in cocktails. This is a good vinegar herb.
The leaves are used for herb tea.

Chervil

This is one of the herbs used by the French in their famous
herb omelette, 'aux fines herbes.' The taste resembles parsley but
is stronger and has a distinctive flavor of its own that goes
especially well with eggs, and also with fish, and in potato and
onion soup. It is good in potato salad.

Chives

Chives can be used in any dish requiring a mild onion flavor.
The tender tops are excellent in fresh green salads, in omelettes,
in soups; and they give a better flavor than common onion to
meat loaf and potato salad.

Cicely, Sweet
Giant Sweet Chervil

The leaves of sweet cicely add an anise flavor to green salads.
The long brown-black seeds add an anise flavor to cooked foods,
and they go well with cabbage. The roots may be cooked as a
potherb.

Costmary
Alecost, Sweet Mary, Bible Leaf

Costmary is used sparingly in green salads and a few poultry
dishes, and in some jellies. The rather large leaves have a very
strong anise flavor.

THyME

Cress, Upland

Upland cress is a tangy salad herb, used either in mixed green salads or alone. Not to be confused with land cress (peppergrass)—a little of which goes a long way—upland cress is quite like water cress in both flavor and appearance, only much larger, with much larger leaves, in fact a giant by comparison with the water herb.

Dill

Dill is known to most people as the herb of dill pickles. It is also an excellent herb to use with fish and lamb. The green sprigs are used for pickles, and also in gravies and sauces, but either the green leaves or the dried seeds are good in cooking.

Garlic

In the hands of the educated cook, garlic can be a gourmet's delight; in the hands of the indiscriminate or the novice, it can be a dining room horror. The safe procedure for a beginner is to rub the salad bowl with a clove of garlic, then remove the clove before serving the salad, or depend upon garlic vinegar or a mixed herb vinegar containing garlic for the flavor of this herb in salads. Bury a clove of garlic in a roast of lamb on a toothpick, and remove the clove before carving the roast so that no unsuspecting guest will receive more garlic flavor than he would wish. After a thorough study of cookery with garlic, the cook will know in which dishes to use this herb generously.

Lovage

Lovage is an herb with an exotic and unusual flavor suggestive of the Orient. The leaves, fresh or dried, can be used liberally in any dish that calls for curry. Because it is not so strong as the Far Eastern spice, one should double the quantity called for in a favorite curry recipe. It is an excellent soup herb.

Marjoram, Sweet

Sweet marjoram is an aromatic leaf herb. It improves almost any recipe with beef—meat loaf, meat balls, steak, and roasts; also sauces for spaghetti, and soups with meat stock.

The flavor of sweet marjoram is similar to, but more delicate than, most species of *Origanum* with which it is often mistakenly identified.

Mint
Spearmint

This is the mint julep herb, the mint of mint sauce for lamb, and also one of the commercial mints of chewing gum fame. It is good with carrots or peas. Used either green or dried in cooking, its cool fresh flavor is quite unlike that which it imparts to gum. Spearmint makes a fine vinegar by itself or, in combination with lemon balm, lemint vinegar, which has a delightful flavor. Spearmint leaves also make a fine herb tea, either alone or combined with regular tea or with the leaves of lemon balm or pennyroyal.

Nasturtiums

The leaves of nasturtiums are peppery and sharp and make a good addition to green salads. The young seeds are pickled.

Origanum

Origanum can be used as a substitute in recipes that call for sweet marjoram. The two herbs taste somewhat different but both lend themselves to the same type of cookery; that is, all beef dishes, meat balls, meat loaf, steaks, and roasts; sauces for spaghetti, soups with beef stock.

Parsley

Parsley, the cook's delight, is so commonly used that one is apt to forget that it is an herb, the term herb often bringing to mind something exotic, rare, and less well known than this common garden plant. Parsley, however, is an herb and a good one, used fresh or dried, in soups, in ragouts; with all meats and every kind of fish that swims in the rivers or the seas; also with eggs, and, in short, with a multitude of recipes for luncheon and dinner.

Pennyroyal

English pennyroyal has a strong distinctive flavor, reminding one slightly of peppermint. It is a famous tea herb, known to

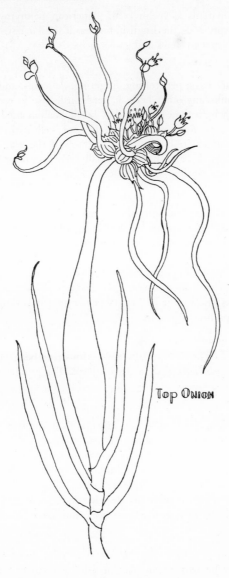

Top Onion

our grandparents as 'pennyry'al.' American pennyroyal is not the same species as the English, but has a similar flavor. Pennyroyal adds zest to stews and game recipes.

Rosemary

Rosemary has a penetrating, lingering, delicious, and unusual flavor, unlike any other herb. It needs little else to recommend it as a fish herb than the fact that Izaak Walton used it in his favorite recipe for cooking trout. It goes well with most fish dishes, whether fresh-water fish or those of the sea. It is also good with pork or veal, and especially with venison. It should be used with caution. A pinch goes a long way.

Sage

Sage is so well known to the American cook that to mention its chief use in the kitchen seems superfluous, for few could roast a Thanksgiving turkey or Sunday chicken without this aromatic herb.

It is a most important herb in making pork sausage, sage cheese, and in stuffing a veal roast. Sage is also a tea herb. As most cooks know, sage has a very penetrating flavor and should be used sparingly.

Savory, Summer

Summer savory is especially good with string beans. It is identified as a fish herb, also good with pork. The pungent flavor is quite strong.

Shallots

This onion from Syria is so superior in flavor that once you have tried the small planting suggested in the plan you will plant ten times the number the next season. If you buy them in the market, the bulbs may be broken into cloves. Take 4 or 5 cloves when the recipe calls for 1 shallot.

Shallots are good with any dish in place of common onions, particularly so with steaks, roast beef, and game.

Tarragon

Tarragon is a most popular kitchen herb. Those who may not know the part it can play in fish cookery are very likely familiar with tarragon vinegar, an excellent salad vinegar for making French dressing, good in horse-radish and other sauces. Also, it is very sympathetic with chicken.

Thyme

Like sage, thyme is appreciated by American cooks and its many uses need hardly be mentioned. A pinch of thyme belongs in most soups, in poultry stuffing, in beef and lamb stews, in chowders, with fresh and smoked pork, in short with almost every meat and many fish dishes. Use sparingly.

ADDITIONAL KITCHEN HERBS

The notes in the next few pages are to introduce the cook to the use of culinary herbs other than the basic twenty-four. For general notes on growing these herbs, see Chapter 6.

Angelica

Angelica is a confectioner's herb. The sweetish stalk may be candied, and the bitter sweet leaves cooked with rhubarb or used in rhubarb pie. The oil of angelica roots and seeds is used for flavoring vermouth and certain liqueurs.

Anise

The seeds of anise are used for breads and cakes, and for flavoring the liqueur anisette. It was prized in the great households of the Middle Ages, among them that of the Emperor Charlemagne.

Bayberry

The bayberry shrub that bears the gray-clustered berries used in making fragrant bayberry candles, can also be of use to the cook—not the berries but the shiny green leaves. They are a substitute for bay leaf (the true bay, *Laurus nobilis*) sold in grocery stores and familiar to all American cooks. A bayberry leaf has a milder flavor than the true bay and can be used generously in all recipes calling for bay leaf, such as soups and ragouts. Bayberry leaves were first used by the colonists who

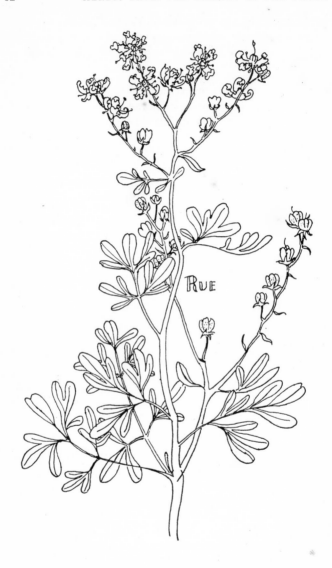

RUE

were seeking substitutes for herbs they had known at home. The culinary species is *Myrica pensylvanica*.

Calamint

This alpine savory is a tea herb. The leaves are used.

Caraway

The seeds of caraway are commonly used for cakes and rye bread. The root is cooked as a potherb. The seeds are also very good in cabbage casseroles and soups, in beet pickles, ragouts, and are used in making caraway cheese. The oil of caraway is used to flavor kümmel, a liqueur.

Celery

Uses of celery with poultry, in soups and stews, in stuffings and sauces, are too well known to mention here, but one fact about celery not known to all cooks is worthy of comment: the dried and pulverized leaves of this herb make an excellent addition to the herb and spice shelf. Use in recipes where celery flavor is called for.

Celery seeds are not set until the second year and are best bought in a store.

Coriander

Coriander is one of the ingredients in curry powder. The round brown seeds have a strong sweetish aromatic taste, which goes very well with game and certain shellfish such as shrimp. It is also a confectioner's herb and used as flavoring in certain liqueurs.

Chicory

The leaves are a welcome addition to green salad in early spring. They make a bitter spinach-like green when cooked.

The roots of chicory are important industrially. They are roasted, and often sold mixed with coffee.

Corn-salad
Lamb's Lettuce, Fetticus

Corn-salad is as mild in flavor as roquette is strong. There is a faint, almost undetectable suggestion of mustard, but no pronounced flavor of any kind in the leaves which can be used with, or instead of, lettuce to mix with other and stronger salad leaves such as those of upland cress, costmary, or nasturtiums. In the seventeenth century, corn-salad leaves were recommended by John Evelyn as a 'sallet of themselves.'

Fennel

Fennel has been known since ancient times as a fish herb. The bulbous lower stems are also used as a potherb. In the past the seeds were taken to church and nibbled during long sermons.

The tender stalks may be served as a green canape.

Geranium (see Pelargonium)

Hops

Hops are known to everyone as an ingredient in brewing malt liquors. At one time, the young shoots were used in salads and as a potherb.

Horehound

For centuries, horehound has been a confectioner's herb, used with honey for making a medicinal candy good for coughs and colds.

Horse-radish

This pungent, hot member of the mustard family has long been considered good for digestion and a stimulant for the appetite. Who could eat oysters without a prepared sauce of grated horse-radish root? It is traditional also with beef. At one time in England it was commonly used as a mutton sauce.

Hyssop

Hyssop is rarely used in the kitchen today, but its use could well be revived. It is an ancient sweet herb, very, very strong. A few leaves give an interesting flavor to green salads and beef soup. The dried flowers are also sometimes used in soups.

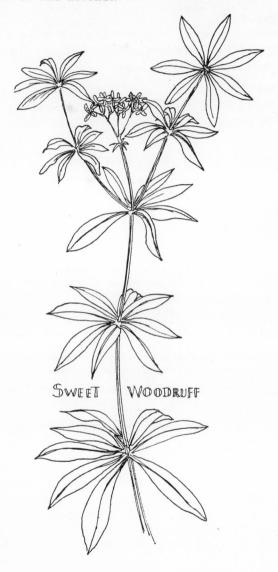

SWEET WOODRUFF

Marigold, Pot
Calendula

The petals are known as an adulterant for saffron. They are also used to season stews and soups.

Mustard

Mustard has been known as a spinach since Dioscorides' day, the first century of the Christian era. Its rather rough bitter leaves are especially good in the spring.

Onions, Top (See also Shallots and Chives)

The large hollow stalks of top onions may be filled with well-seasoned cottage or cream cheese and used like celery as a canape. The bulbs of the top onion may be used in the spring like common onions.

Pelargonium, Rose
Rose Geranium

The leaves of the rose pelargonium are commonly used in making apple jelly.

Rhubarb
Pie-plant

The acid leaf stalks of rhubarb have been known for many years for their use as sauce and for making rhubarb pie.

Rocombole
Giant Garlic

Rocombole is a mild-flavored garlic, used for any recipe that calls for garlic.

Roquette, or Rocket-salad

Roquette is a very strong-flavored herb used in France both as a salad and a potherb.

Writing in the year 1699, John Evelyn recommended it highly for salads. In his opinion, it should never be left out, 'especially where there is much lettuce.' This advice is sound. The flavor is heavy and quite exotic. Use very little, and always the young

SKIRRET

leaves, in a mixed green salad. When old or grown too slowly, roquette is tough and unpalatable.

Rue

Rue is a medieval salad herb, and used with fish and eggs. The Italians sometimes use rue for salads today but most gardeners do not care to harvest this herb. Some people develop a skin irritation on contact with the plant.

Rue is also a vinegar herb.

Safflower

The oil is in common use in India. The flowers are used as a substitute for saffron.

Saffron

The cooks of the Middle Ages used saffron often for both flavor and a yellow coloring matter. It is used today in Spanish dishes.

It is important in the fish recipe, bouillabaisse. The extract is sometimes used for coloring liqueurs, cakes, sauces.

Samphire

In seventeenth-century England, the leaves and young stems of samphire, which grows on the cliffs of Dover, were pickled. Today anyone living on the coast of Massachusetts or along the coast a few hundred miles to the south can find wild samphire, often called glasswort, but this is not the culinary species, however.

Savory, Winter

Winter savory has a very strong, dominant, and rather overpowering flavor, similar to, but inferior to, summer savory.

Sesame
Bene

The oil of sesame is commonly used in India for cooking. In Europe, it is an adulterant for olive oil. Confectioners like it, and the seeds are popular for breads and cakes.

SAFFLOWER

Skirret

Skirret is an ancient potherb said to be so popular with the Emperor Tiberius that 'he accepted them for Tribute.' (John Evelyn)

The roots should be dug in spring or fall, and the woody core cut out before cooking.

The flavor of the roots is sweetish. John Evelyn, writing in the *Acetaria,* said they were excellent 'being boil'd, stew'd, roasted under the Embers, bak'd in pies, whole, sliced or in pulp—'

Tansy

The flowers and leaves of tansy are for tea. Tansy was liked in colonial days not only for tea but also for puddings and cakes.

Woodruff, Sweet

Sweet woodruff, the waldmeister of Germany, is famous in that country for its use as a flavoring in May wine.

5

Recipes from Hemlock Hill Herb Farm

'A handful of sliced Horseradish roots, with a handsome little fagot of Rosemary, Thyme, and Winter Savoury.'

Izaak Walton, 1676 (for trout).

THE RECIPES that follow originated in our kitchen and require only the twenty-four basic culinary herbs, and dried celery, bay leaf, horse-radish, and a few spices. After trying these recipes, a cook can then apply her knowledge of the use of herbs to some favorite recipes of her own.

Measuring

All measurements, teaspoons, et cetera, are level.

We give quantities in the recipes for all ingredients except the fat used for frying, and, in most cases, salt and pepper. The former depends upon how much fat you like in your food, and the latter upon individual taste. Some like dishes hot and salty, others like a mere sprinkle of salt and pepper.

Below is a list of home products that anyone who has followed the directions so far will have on the kitchen shelf. We are assuming that the cook has sown and grown, harvested and dried herbs, and made at least one herb vinegar.

Note: Herbs in the recipes are dried and pulverized unless otherwise stated.

HERB SHELF: YOUR OWN PRODUCTS

DRIED LEAF HERBS

			SEEDS
Balm, lemon	Marjoram	Rosemary	Cicely, Sweet
Basil	Mint	Sage	Dill
Chervil	Origanum	Savory, Summer	
Chives	Parsley	Tarragon	
Lovage	Pennyroyal	Thyme	

HERB VINEGARS   IN THE CELLAR

Basil	Lemint	Garlic
Burnet, Salad	Mixed Herbs	Shallots
Garlic	Tarragon	

MEATS: From a Gourmet's Hamburger to the Sunday Roast

GOURMET'S HAMBURGER

1 pound ground beef
1 teaspoon marjoram or origanum
¼ teaspoon dried chives or 1 teaspoon chopped fresh
½ teaspoon parsley
16 pickled nasturtium seeds or capers
salt and pepper to taste
butter or oleomargarine

Mix beef and herbs, salt and pepper, and pat into 4 plump hamburgers. Make a small hole in the center of each, insert 4 nasturtium seeds or capers. Press meat back over the seeds. Fry over a hot fire in butter or oleomargarine.

YANKEE STEAK

1 pound ground beef
⅓ of a green pepper
3 shallots or 1 onion
1 slice bread
1 egg
1 tablespoon milk
1 teaspoon parsley
½ teaspoon marjoram
¼ teaspoon thyme
¼ teaspoon celery
salt and pepper to taste
butter or oleomargarine

Crumble the bread and mix with milk and the egg. Mince the green pepper and the shallots. Add, with the herbs and meat. Mix all ingredients well together with salt and pepper to taste. Pat into 4 hamburgers and fry over a quick fire. Do not over-cook.

MEAT BALLS

2 pounds ground beef	3 teaspoons parsley
3 eggs	1 cup finely cut chives
5 slices bread	¼ teaspoon thyme
2 tablespoons milk	1 teaspoon salt
1½ teaspoons marjoram or origanum	½ teaspoon pepper
	butter or oleomargarine

Break the eggs into the milk, crumble and soak the bread; add the beef, herbs, salt, and pepper, and mix well. Roll into balls about the size of golf balls. Pre-heat a heavy iron skillet, add butter or oleomargarine for frying. When the fat begins to sizzle, nearly cover the bottom of the pan with meat balls. Do not crowd. Sauté over a hot fire, shaking the pan and touching lightly now and then with a fork so that the meat balls keep turning. Fry until the meat balls are brown. Serve in a casserole with meat ball gravy.

MEAT BALL GRAVY

drippings in skillet after meat balls are removed	1 teaspoon paprika
3 shallots, chopped	3 teaspoons flour
1½ teaspoons celery	1 teaspoon sugar
1 teaspoon parsley	2 teaspoons sherry
1 pinch pennyroyal	1 cup sour cream
	salt and pepper to taste

Sauté the shallots in the drippings until they start turning pale yellow. Mix sugar, the herbs, and 1 teaspoon of flour together, and add. Cook until brown, not burned. Mix remaining 2 teaspoons flour with the cream, and add with the paprika. When gravy starts thickening, add sherry, salt, and pepper.

MEAT LOAF

same ingredients as for meat
  balls
4 strips bacon

1 green pepper
paprika
butter or oleomargarine

Mix the same ingredients called for in meat ball recipe and
shape into a loaf in a well-greased casserole or pie plate. Cut
green pepper into thin strips and press gently into top of meat
loaf. Sprinkle with paprika. Halve the bacon strips, and lay
them over the loaf. Bake in a moderate oven and serve hot or
cold.

SPAGHETTI AND MEAT BALLS

1 package spaghetti
meat balls (see meat ball recipe)

grated cheese
spaghetti sauce (see below)

SPAGHETTI SAUCE

1 cup fresh or dried mushrooms
1 teaspoon brown sugar
1 clove garlic
2 teaspoons lovage
1 teaspoon paprika
1 tomato
1 tablespoon flour
1½ teaspoons grated cheese

1 cup milk
1 tablespoon butter
2 tablespoons beef drippings
  (from meat balls, steak, or
  roast beef)
salt and pepper to taste
2 cups water

Place beef drippings and butter in the frying pan; when siz-
zling hot add brown sugar, stirring constantly, let nearly come
to a burn. Stir in 2 cups water. Slice the mushrooms, chop the
tomato, mince the clove of garlic, and add these with the lovage,
the paprika, and the cheese. Slowly blend flour into the milk,
then stir it into the ingredients in the frying pan. Let come to
a boil, stirring constantly until of right consistency. Sprinkle
with salt and pepper to taste. If there is not enough liquid, add
more milk and let simmer.

Serve with meat balls and with spaghetti cooked according to the standard recipe given on the spaghetti box, and grated cheese.

KÅLDOLMAR

same ingredients as for meat balls
1 large cabbage
½ teaspoon pulverized dill or sweet cicely seeds

salt to taste
butter, oleomargarine, or chicken fat
2 teaspoons flour

Carefully remove 16 large leaves from the cabbage head. Wilt the leaves by pouring boiling water over them. Save the water.

Prepare the recipe for meat balls, add dill or sweet cicely, and pat into rolls about the size of small buns. Fold a wilted cabbage leaf around each meat bun. Secure the leaf with 2 toothpicks, or tie with string.

Place the cabbage rolls in a buttered casserole or a Dutch oven, and brown them in the oven but do not let them burn. When the rolls are brown, blend flour with 1½ cups of the water in which cabbage leaves were wilted. Salt to taste. Cook until sauce thickens, basting continuously.

SIRLOIN STEAK SUPREME
Over the Coals

3 pound sirloin steak
1 teaspoon parsley
½ teaspoon marjoram
½ cup butter
salt and pepper to taste

1 bag charcoal
pitcher of water
fireplace
long-handled grill

Let steak stand at room temperature about a half hour before cooking. If the steak is frozen, be certain that it is thoroughly thawed. Cut through the fat around the edge of the steak with a sharp knife at intervals of about a quarter inch. This will make it possible for the fat to cook brown and crisp. If the steak does not appear to be tender, puncture the meat (do not cut) in about a dozen places with the point of a knife.

Melt the butter and mix in the marjoram and parsley, and set near the fire to keep liquid.

Secure the steak in the grill. By now your charcoal fire should be glowing. Hold the steak close enough to the coals to sear it, then turn and broil the other side, and salt and pepper both sides. By this time the fat dripping from the steak will have caused the coals to burst into flames. Hold the steak aside a moment while you dash about a half pint of water over the fire to dim it; then continue to broil the steak over the now softly glowing coals until it is rare, medium or well-done, as suits your taste. Carve and serve with the melted butter and herbs.

KIDNEY AUX FINES HERBES

1 young beef kidney
3 shallots (about 12 cloves)
1 green pepper
1 bunch carrots
¼ pound mushrooms
2 medium potatoes
1 tomato
3 sprigs parsley
2 stalks celery
2 tablespoons herb vinegar with garlic

1 sprig marjoram
1 sprig thyme
2 teaspoons paprika
1 tablespoon sherry
½ teaspoon lemon juice
1 tablespoon flour
salt and pepper to taste
butter or oleomargarine

Remove fat and sinew from kidney. Cut in about ¾-inch pieces and wash. Then soak kidney in vinegar and enough salted water to cover it for at least an hour. Pare the potatoes and cut in small pieces. Scrape and dice carrots. Remove seeds and stems and slice green pepper into thin strips. Cut mushroom stems from cap, and cut up the stems. Slice the tomato. Cut up the celery in small pieces. Now boil all the vegetables, except the mushrooms.

Drain kidney and sauté in butter or oleomargarine in the lower half of a Dutch oven for about five minutes. Do not over-cook. Meanwhile chop herbs fine (aux fines herbes). Mix the flour with ½ cup of cold vegetable stock. Add the mushrooms, vegetables, herbs, lemon juice, sherry, and flour water. Cover the Dutch oven and let simmer until juice thickens—about five minutes.

If you make this recipe in the winter, you may substitute the following dried herb measurements: ½ teaspoon marjoram, 1 pinch of thyme, 2 teaspoons parsley.

LIVER EN CASSEROLE

1 pound calf's liver or beef liver, sliced	1 teaspoon paprika
	½ teaspoon basil
1 bunch carrots	1 teaspoon parsley
½ pound mushrooms	¼ teaspoon lovage
2 shallots or 2 medium onions	1 teaspoon mustard seeds
4 slices bacon	1 tablespoon sherry
2 cups tomato juice	salt and pepper to taste
1 tablespoon flour	2 teaspoons flour

Cut carrots in half inch pieces and parboil. Cover bottom of a flat casserole with about ⅓ cup of water but not enough to cover the liver. Wipe liver and sprinkle with salt and pepper and place in casserole. Cover with bacon strips. Bake in medium oven until bacon begins to crisp.

Meanwhile mix flour with herbs and mustard seeds and blend with tomato juice and sherry. Slice shallots and mushrooms. Smother liver with shallots. Place parboiled carrots to one side of the liver and mushrooms on the other side. Pour on tomato juice with the herbs. Bake about ½ hour in moderate oven.

MUSTARD SAUCE

½ cup beef stock	1 teaspoon sherry
¼ teaspoon marjoram	1 teaspoon flour
2 teaspoons mustard flour	salt to taste
¼ teaspoon tarragon vinegar	

Mix ingredients together. Heat and let simmer until the sauce thickens. Serve with pot roast or boiled beef.

RAGOUT HEMLOCK HILL

2 pounds beef
2 shallots or 1 onion
1 clove garlic
1 green pepper
¼ teaspoon thyme
¼ teaspoon pennyroyal
½ teaspoon marjoram or origa-
    num
¼ pint sour cream
5 small tomatoes

½ teaspoon peppercorns
1½ bay leaf
1 teaspoon parsley
1 teaspoon mustard seeds
2 teaspoons paprika
flour
butter or oleomargarine
1 tablespoon sherry
salt and pepper to taste

Peel, slice, and crush clove of garlic in a Dutch oven or casserole with cover. Rub the oven or casserole with the crushed
garlic, then remove and discard. Cut the beef in 1-inch cubes,
roll in flour and brown in butter on top of stove. Then add
peppercorns, mustard seeds, salt, and pepper, and about an inch
of water. Cover and simmer in a slow oven until meat is tender,
adding water if necessary. Next add sliced shallots. When shallots are done, remove meat from stock, pour sour cream into
stock, and heat over a slow fire, stirring constantly until cream
is smooth. Add sherry, herbs, and paprika. Return meat to pan.
Remove stems and seeds and slice pepper; slice the tomatoes and
garnish the ragout. Return to the oven without cover and heat
until gravy commences to bubble.

Serve with green peas, mushrooms, and mint carrots.

TONGUE AU VIN ROUGE

1 smoked beef tongue
½ cup currants
12 cloves
1 teaspoon parsley
1 teaspoon mint
¼ teaspoon basil
¼ teaspoon summer savory
1 teaspoon lemon balm

1 tablespoon pickled nasturtium
    seeds (or capers)
1 teaspoon mustard flour
1 teaspoon lemon juice
2 cups red wine
2 teaspoons sugar
pepper to taste
1 tablespoon nasturtium vinegar
    (or caper)

Soak tongue overnight in 1½ cups red wine diluted with about 1 cup water. Discard this wine and water because it will be too salty to use again. Boil tongue in fresh water until tender, about 2½ hours. Remove from stove and skin; cut off tough root end. Parts of the root end can be saved to grind for sandwich meat.

Now place tongue in flat casserole, rub in the dried herbs, sugar, and mustard, stick with the cloves. Mix the remaining wine (½ cup), nasturtium vinegar, lemon juice, nasturtium seeds, and currants. Roast until brown, basting frequently. If too dry, add a little water.

LAMB CHOPS

4 lamb chops	flour
1 tablespoon olive oil	butter or oleomargarine
1 teaspoon mint	salt and pepper to taste
½ teaspoon chervil	

Wipe lamb chops dry with paper towels. Smear with olive oil. Mix herbs with salt and pepper and rub into meat. Roll in flour. Fry in butter or oleomargarine.

ROAST LAMB AUX SHALLOTS

leg of lamb	1 pinch rosemary
suet, about 4 thin strips	1 clove garlic
12 small peeled potatoes	1 teaspoon lemon juice
12 shallots	olive oil
2 teaspoons mint	flour
1 teaspoon ground dill seeds	salt and pepper to taste
2 teaspoons lemon balm	butter or oleomargarine
2 teaspoons parsley	

Cut one edge of clove of garlic with a knife and rub the roasting pan with clove. Then grease pan. Wipe meat with clean cloth. Set in roasting pan. Smear the top of the roast with olive oil. Let stand at room temperature for a few minutes. Then rub in the herbs and a little flour. Lay strips of suet on top of meat and add a half inch water to pan. Sprinkle the meat with the lemon juice.

Roast in a hot oven, basting regularly, and allowing about 35 minutes to the pound. When nearly done, place the shallots and potatoes around the roast. When basting, roll the vegetables in the gravy. If necessary add a little more water. Serve with lemint sauce.

LEMINT SAUCE
(Lemon Balm and Mint)

¼ cup lemint vinegar   5 teaspoons dark brown sugar or
                                          10 tablespoons honey

Mix vinegar with sugar or honey and let come slowly to a boil.

PORK ASPIC

2 9-ounce jars, boneless pigs feet,   ¼ cup sliced shallots
   packed in vinegar   2 packages unflavored gelatine
3 sprigs fresh parsley   2 cups boiling water
1 sprig fresh dill   1 cup cold liquid (vinegar from
1 pinch rosemary   jars with water added if neces-
½ teaspoon basil   sary)

Cut the fresh parsley and dill fine. Mix with shallots and dried herbs. Dissolve gelatine in the cold liquid. Add the herbs and hot water. Pour into mold, let cool, then chill in the refrigerator until the gelatine begins to set. Add pigs feet and keep mold in refrigerator until the aspic stiffens.

PORK CHOPS
Dutch Oven

2 pork chops   1 pinch thyme
1 apple   1 pinch sage
2 pinches rosemary   2 teaspoons flour
¼ teaspoon basil   butter or oleomargarine
                                          salt and pepper to taste

With a sharp knife, cut fat on edge of chops to the meat at
¼-inch intervals. Mix flour with herbs, salt, and pepper. Roll
chops in flour and herbs and the condiments. Brown over hot
fire on both sides, then add ¼ cup water. Cover and cook thoroughly. When nearly done, core and slice apple and drop into
pan. Cook until apple slices are soft.

HAM AU VIN ROUGE

half a pre-cooked ham, about 6 pounds	1 teaspoon cinnamon
2 cups claret wine	1 teaspoon tarragon
½ cup brown sugar	1 teaspoon basil
2 teaspoons herb vinegar, or basil or garlic vinegar	¼ teaspoon thyme
1 teaspoon mustard	¼ teaspoon rosemary
	cloves
	flour

If the ham is not pre-cooked, parboil in water for several
hours or until tender; remove skin if any.

Set ham in covered stainless steel kettle or earthenware crock
with wine and let marinate overnight. Save wine. Remove ham
and dot generously with cloves. Set the ham fat side up in a
roasting pan. Rub in the herbs. Mix brown sugar with vinegar
and spread over tops and sides of the ham. Sprinkle with the
mustard and cinnamon. Place in hot oven with wine in which
the ham was marinated, and add enough water to make about
½ inch liquid in the pan. When ham begins to brown, lower
oven heat to medium. Baste as needed. Roasting time about 1
hour.

HAM EN CASSEROLE

1 cup left-over ham, put through grinder	½ green pepper
½ package macaroni (pound package)	1 tomato
	2 teaspoons chopped chives
½ cup sharp store cheese or grated cheese	½ teaspoon basil
	1 cup sour cream
2 eggs	bread crumbs
	butter or oleomargarine

Break up macaroni and cook in boiling salted water, as directed on package. Break up cheese in small pieces. Cut pepper and tomato into thin slices. Mix together with a fork the basil, eggs, and sour cream. Grease a two-quart casserole. First place a layer of cooked macaroni on bottom, then a layer of ham, one of cheese, one of pepper, repeating until all the ingredients are used. Top with tomato and chives, pour on eggs and cream. Sprinkle with crumbs, dot with butter or oleomargarine, and bake in a medium oven until brown.

HERB MUSTARD
Serve with ham

¼ cup mustard flour	4 teaspoons mixed Herb Vinegar
1 teaspoon salt	No. 1 (see Chapter 3)
¼ teaspoon sugar	3 teaspoons white wine
	1 pinch rosemary

Blend ingredients, and keep under refrigeration in a closed jar.

CHICKEN IN A DUTCH OVEN

1 fowl (5–6 lb.)	½ bay leaf or 2 bayberry leaves
2 shallots or 1 onion	¼ teaspoon sage
2 stalks celery	⅛ teaspoon lovage
½ green pepper	paprika, salt, and pepper
3 sprigs fresh parsley	flour
½ cup sour cream	

Have butcher cut up fowl for fricassee. If the bird is very fat, remove excess fat and render for use in frying. Wing tips and neck may also be removed and boiled for soup. Roll other parts in flour; salt and pepper them; place in a Dutch oven with about a half an inch of water. Cover and bake in a medium oven or on top of stove until chicken starts to get tender. Then dice celery, shallots, and green pepper and add with the herbs. Cover again and cook until chicken is tender. Remove cover and bake in the oven of your stove until brown. Add sour cream; baste thoroughly; spray lightly with paprika; and leave in oven until gravy thickens.

CHICKEN LIVERS WITH RICE

1 pound chicken livers	⅓ teaspoon thyme
1 cup rice	¼ teaspoon basil
2 shallots or 1 onion	2 teaspoons lovage
1½ cups mashed fresh tomatoes	butter or oleomargarine
or canned tomatoes	flour
2 stalks celery	salt and pepper to taste
4 mushrooms	

Cook rice in your favorite way or according to directions on package.

Roll the chicken livers in flour, sprinkle with salt and pepper, and sauté in butter, about 3 minutes. Remove livers from the pan. Chop the shallots, dice the celery, slice the mushrooms, and sauté. Return liver to pan with tomatoes and herbs. Cook until ingredients are well blended. Serve with rice.

SAVORY ROAST CHICKEN

1 roasting chicken (6 lbs.)	⅛ teaspoon basil
giblets	¼ teaspoon thyme
5 slices bread	⅛ teaspoon sage
1 egg	1 teaspoon celery
½ pound mushrooms	1 teaspoon parsley
3 green peppers	¼ teaspoon summer savory
½ cup sherry	½ cup water
1 tablespoon milk	salt and pepper to taste
flour	

Boil giblets in water until tender. Remove from water and mince. Save stock for gravy.

Prepare the stuffing as follows. Put shallots through coarse grind in meat grinder, then grind the bread which will absorb the onion juice in the grinder. Mix shallots, bread, egg, and milk together with salt and pepper and herbs, omitting the summer savory. Stuff chicken and skewer or sew opening at tail

end. Thrust neck into opening at head end and skewer or sew.
Then tie the legs and wings to the body with string.

Now roll chicken in flour and sprinkle with pepper and salt.
Any excess chicken fat should be cut in thin slices and placed
on breast of roast. Set chicken in roasting pan with giblet stock.
Roast in hot oven until flour shows signs of browning. Slice
mushrooms; remove stems and seeds, and slice green peppers,
and add to roasting pan with summer savory and sherry and
water. Reduce heat and roast until tender, basting frequently.

CHICKEN GRAVY

4 tablespoons chicken fat	2 teaspoons parsley
4 tablespoons flour	1 teaspoon paprika
½ cup chicken stock	1 pinch rosemary
½ cup cream	1 pinch sage
½ teaspoon sugar	salt and pepper to taste
½ teaspoon thyme	minced giblets

Mix cream slowly into 3 tablespoons flour and set aside. Heat
chicken fat in frying pan over hot fire, add sugar and the remaining flour, stirring constantly. When brown add cream and
stock, giblets, herbs, salt, pepper, and paprika, and let simmer
over fire, stirring constantly until gravy is of desired consistency.

VEAL CUTLETS AUX HERBES

4 veal cutlets	¼ teaspoon rosemary
4 anchovy fillets	½ teaspoon marjoram or origa-
1 egg	num
bread crumbs	4 slices lemon
12 pickled nasturtium seeds or	salt and pepper to taste
capers	butter or oleomargarine
½ teaspoon tarragon	

Pound the cutlets with a wooden potato masher. Mix salt and
pepper with herbs and rub into both sides of the cutlets. Whip
the egg with a fork lightly and roll the cutlets first in the egg,
then in bread crumbs. Sauté in butter or oleomargarine over a
medium fire until done. Serve with a slice of lemon on each

and top the lemon with an anchovy ringed around 4 nasturtium seeds.

FINNY FISH AND SHELLFISH

CODFISH CHOWDER

1 pound fillet fresh cod	1 teaspoon tarragon
5 medium-sized potatoes	1 teaspoon thyme
3 shallots or 2 medium-sized onions	½ teaspoon summer savory
	dab of butter
2 stalks celery	salt and pepper to taste
1 cup milk	

Make sure the bones have all been removed from the fillet. Cut the fish in small pieces. Peel and dice the potatoes. Ring the shallots. Chop celery in about ½-inch pieces. Boil the shallots, celery, potatoes, the herbs, salt, and pepper in a pint of water until the potatoes are nearly done. Add fish and let boil about five minutes, then pour in milk and let come to boiling point. Add dab of butter and serve.

EELS IN ASPIC

¾ pound fresh eel	10 peppercorns
2 envelopes unflavored gelatine	⅛ teaspoon rosemary
2½ cups eel stock, boiling hot	1 pinch thyme
2 cups cold stock	1 teaspoon lemon juice
2 bay leaves or 4 bayberry	lemon peelings from a quarter of
2 sprigs fresh dill, or 2 teaspoons dried	a lemon

Pare off the very outer skin of the lemon in small pieces. Boil eel in 5 cups water until done. Cool. Bone eel and cut in ¾-inch pieces. Chop the fresh dill and mix with the thyme, rosemary, peppercorns, bay leaves, lemon juice, and hot eel stock. Dissolve the gelatine in the cold stock. Blend stocks together and pour into a chilled mold. Let cool, place in refrigerator until aspic starts to set. Then add the lemon peelings and the eel, and chill until the aspic stiffens.

LUNCHEON KIPPERS

1 can kippered herring (12 oz.)	1 teaspoon tarragon vinegar
½ cup milk	⅛ teaspoon rosemary
1 tablespoon flour	butter or oleomargarine

Melt butter or oleomargarine in frying pan. Sauté the herring quickly. Blend a little milk into the flour, then add the remaining milk, tarragon vinegar, and rosemary. Pour over herring with the juice in the can. Let sauce thicken, and serve.

KIPPERED HERRING AU JUS

2 kippered herring (not canned)	1 tablespoon tarragon vinegar
⅔ cup milk	1 tablespoon sherry
½ lemon	2 shallots or 1 onion
¼ teaspoon summer savory	flour
¼ teaspoon parsley	dab of butter or oleomargarine

Stir sherry into milk. Dip herring in vinegar, turning until they are coated. Let marinate two or three minutes. Rinse in water. Roll herring in flour and place them skin side down in a buttered casserole. Sprinkle with the herbs, top with shallots sliced thin, then squeeze the lemon juice over the fish. Bake in medium oven. When nearly done, or when shallots are slightly brown, pour on the milk and sherry. When sauce begins to thicken, baste, then remove from oven, and serve with dill potatoes.

SALMON COUNTRY STYLE

1 pound canned salmon	½ teaspoon celery
2 slices bacon	1 teaspoon lemon juice
2 shallots or 1 onion	paprika
1 pinch tarragon	sprig of sweet cicely or parsley
1 pinch rosemary	

Remove the salmon from can in one piece. Discard the salty juice. Place in flat casserole or on a pie plate, with approximately ¼-inch water. Press salmon gently down to flatten it a trifle. Cut the bacon slices in half, rub the herbs on both sides of the bacon, and cover the top of the salmon with the bacon strips.

Cut shallots into rings and scatter on top of bacon. Cook in a hot oven and baste regularly to prevent drying. About five minutes before removing from oven, sprinkle with lemon juice and paprika. If it is summer time, garnish with fresh chopped sweet cicely leaves. In winter use parsley.

SALMON STEAK

1 pound salmon steak	1 sprig parsley, chopped fine
1 pinch rosemary	oleomargarine or chicken fat
1/4 teaspoon tarragon	butter
1/4 teaspoon lemon balm	salt and pepper to taste
1 slice lemon to each piece salmon	

Grease a casserole with oleomargarine or chicken fat. Sprinkle the salmon on both sides with the dried herbs, salt, and pepper. Place the salmon in the casserole and dot the topside with butter. Broil, or fry quickly on top of stove, first one side, then the other. Serve with a slice of lemon on each piece of fish and parsley with melted butter.

SHAD ROE

1 pound shad roe	4 slices bacon
1 egg	1 teaspoon lemon juice
1 tablespoon milk	flour
1 teaspoon parsley	butter or oleomargarine
1/2 teaspoon summer savory	salt and pepper to taste

Beat the egg and mix together with milk and herbs, salt, and pepper. Roll roe in flour, then dip in egg, and roll again in flour. Lay roe in greased pan with bacon strips on top. Sprinkle on the lemon juice. Bake in moderate oven until roe is brown.

SHRIMP ASPIC

1 pound uncooked shrimp	4 thin slices lemon
1/2 cup white wine	2 teaspoons whole dill seeds
2 teaspoons tarragon vinegar	1 teaspoon summer savory
1 medium green pepper	1 teaspoon parsley
3 envelopes unflavored gelatine	1 teaspoon salt

Boil the shrimp in salted water with dill seeds, parsley, and summer savory and tarragon vinegar for about fifteen minutes. Remove the shrimp; remove stem and seeds and slice pepper; add the pepper to stock and boil about 3 minutes, or until pepper wilts. Cool. Shell the shrimp, making sure to remove the black vein from the back of each. Cut shrimp in ½-inch pieces, and put back into the pot with 3 cups shrimp stock, and the white wine. Heat on stove. Meanwhile, dissolve the gelatine in 1½ cups cool stock (if there is not enough stock, add water).

As the shrimps come to a boil, remove pot from stove, add cool stock with the gelatine, and pour into a chilled mold. Decorate with lemon slices, and when cool place in refrigerator to set.

SHRIMP LEVISTICUM

1 pound uncooked shrimp	3 sprigs fresh dill or 1 teaspoon
1 can bean sprouts with juice	dill seeds or ground dill
¼ pound mushrooms	½ teaspoon summer savory
2 shallots or 1 onion	1 teaspoon paprika
2 stalks celery	1 teaspoon tarragon vinegar
1 green pepper	3 or 4 grains cayenne pepper
4 teaspoons lovage (levisticum)	butter or oleomargarine
	salt and pepper to taste

Boil shrimp in salted water with dill about 15 minutes. When cool, remove shells and also the small black veins which are harmless but do not look attractive. Place tarragon vinegar in dish in which shrimp are to be served. Roll the shrimp in the vinegar. If shrimp are jumbo, cut into halves or quarters. Leave small shrimp whole. Boil the bean sprouts in their own juice about 10 minutes. Do not overcook. Remove from fire and keep warm.

The sauce is made as follows. Cut celery in ¼-inch pieces; remove stem and seeds and cut pepper in thin slices; cut off lower half of mushroom stems and save them for soup, slicing caps and remaining stems. Slice shallots in rings and sauté them in butter or oleomargarine until they soften. Spoon onions to one side of frying pan and add the mushrooms. Sauté onions and mushrooms until onions are golden brown. By this time the mushrooms should be done. Add celery, green pepper, the paprika, cayenne, herbs, and salt and pepper to taste. Add the juice in which the bean sprouts cooked and let simmer about 15 minutes, or until the liquid is reduced to the right consistency. Pour the sauce over the shrimp, and serve with the bean sprouts and rice, and soya sauce if desired.

PICKLED SMELTS

2 dozen smelts	1 teaspoon salt
1 cup flour	¼ teaspoon pepper
1 egg	½ teaspoon tarragon
1 cup tarragon vinegar	⅛ teaspoon rosemary
	butter or oleomargarine

Gut the smelts, remove fins and tails. Mix together flour, herbs, salt, and pepper. Beat egg with a fork. Roll smelts first in flour, then in egg, and then in flour again. Fry in butter or oleomargarine in hot pan until brown, turning frequently. Place in casserole, and pour the tarragon vinegar over the hot smelts. Let cool and marinate for at least 12 hours.

SWORDFISH SUPREME

1 pound swordfish steak	1 teaspoon lemon juice
1 sprig of parsley	salt and pepper to taste
⅛ teaspoon rosemary	2 tablespoons butter
¼ teaspoon tarragon	

Broil swordfish until golden brown. Melt butter in saucepan and stir in lemon juice, herbs, salt, and pepper. Pour over the fish and serve immediately. Garnish with chopped parsley.

TARRAGON SAUCE FOR FISH

1 cup milk	3 teaspoons flour
3 teaspoons lemon juice	½ teaspoon tarragon
2 teaspoons pickled nasturtium	1 hard-boiled egg
seeds or capers	salt and pepper to taste

Stir the flour into ¼ cup milk until well blended, add the remaining milk. Add tarragon, nasturtium seeds, lemon juice, salt, and pepper. Heat over a slow fire, stirring constantly, until sauce is of right consistency. Chop the hard-boiled egg and blend with sauce. Serve with boiled or sautéed fish; especially good with haddock, cod, or halibut.

EGGS AND HERBS

EGGS IN NESTS

left-over spinach or beet greens	chervil
4 eggs	salt and pepper to taste

Place left-over greens in a casserole; make 4 depressions in the greens, and break an egg into each. Sprinkle lightly with chervil, salt, and pepper. Cook in medium oven until eggs are done.

HERB OMELET

4 eggs	¼ teaspoon tarragon
4 tablespoons milk	¼ teaspoon basil
¼ teaspoon parsley	salt and pepper to taste
¼ teaspoon chives	butter
¼ teaspoon chervil	

Lightly beat the eggs and milk together with the herbs and salt and pepper. Butter a heavy skillet. Pre-heat over a medium-hot fire until the butter begins to sizzle but not brown. Pour egg mixture into pan, and while eggs cook, keep circling the outer edge with a spatula or a flexible-bladed knife, now and then tipping the pan slightly to let the excess liquid in the center roll under the edge of the omelet. When the liquid is almost gone, leave the omelet untouched for about a minute. Then tip the pan away from you and with a cake turner, fold the nearer half upon the other half. Remove from pan and serve immediately. Herb omelet is good when made with either dry or fresh chopped herbs.

MUSHROOM OMELET

4 eggs	¼ teaspon parsley
1 cup milk	¼ teaspoon basil
¼ pound mushrooms	salt and pepper to taste
1 teaspoon flour	butter

Cut off mushroom stems and save for soup. Slice caps into well-buttered frying pan. Sauté. Mix flour with ½ cup milk and pour over mushrooms. Stir until sauce thickens. Set aside.

Now beat the eggs together with ½ cup milk, herbs, salt, and pepper. Butter heavy frying pan and pre-heat. Roll the skillet so that the butter is well up on the sides. Pour in eggs and cook until eggs begin to thicken. Spread the mushrooms and sauce on the far side of the pan, on top of half the omelet. Place in hot oven. When the eggs stiffen, fold the omelet over the mushrooms. Leave in the oven about a minute. Serve immediately.

TONGUE OR HAM OMELET

1 cup left-over tongue (or ham)	pinch pepper
4 eggs	no salt; smoked tongue is very
4 tablespoons milk	salty
¼ teaspoon basil	butter
½ teaspoon chervil	

If you are using the back end of a tongue, be sure to remove the small bones. Then grind meat. With a fork beat eggs together with milk, herbs, and pepper. Pre-heat skillet with butter. Be sure sides of skillet are well greased. Pour in eggs. Cover pan. Let cook until eggs start to thicken. Then spread tongue or ham to fit over one half the omelet. Tip pan away from you. Fold omelet over meat. Again cover and let cook about a minute. Serve immediately.

SALADS: Green and Leafy, and Others

CRESS SALAD

upland cress in amount equal to	2 sprigs sweet cicely
a head of lettuce	2 young leaves costmary
⅛ cup chives	1 cucumber

Wash salad leaves and dry thoroughly. Strip leaves of cress off lower stems. With kitchen scissors, cut fine the sweet cicely and the costmary. Chop the chives. Peel and dice the cucumber.

Toss and serve with herb French dressing. This salad has a special tang.

GREEN HERB SALAD #1

2 leaves costmary	2 sprigs sweet cicely
2 sprigs lemon balm	½ green pepper
1 sprig tarragon	½ cucumber
⅓ cup chopped chives	2 stalks celery
2 young borage leaves	½ head cos lettuce

Wash salad leaves and dry thoroughly. Tear the lettuce leaves into fairly small pieces. Peel and dice cucumber. Slice pepper thin. Cut celery stalks in small pieces. Strip leaves of herbs from stems. Snip up costmary, balm, and borage and sweet cicely leaves. Toss all ingredients together, and serve with herb French salad dressing.

GREEN HERB SALAD #2

small head Boston lettuce	½ green pepper
6 leaves cos lettuce	1 plant corn salad
6 sprigs salad burnet	2 young leaves roquette
leaves from 1 plant cress	

Wash lettuce and herbs and dry thoroughly. If weather is warm, chill in refrigerator. Strip leaves from salad burnet, discarding stems. Strip cress leaves. Pull lettuce and cos leaves apart by hand. Cut up fine the corn salad leaves and roquette. The corn salad adds a faint mustard flavor, the roquette an exotic taste.

Serve with herb French salad dressing.

HERB FRENCH SALAD DRESSING #1

3 teaspoons salt	½ teaspoon sugar
¾ teaspoon pepper	½ teaspoon mustard flour
¾ teaspoon paprika	olive oil
1 cup herb vinegar	
1 clove garlic, unless there is garlic in vinegar	

The vinegar may be any of those listed in Chapter 3. Tarragon or garlic vinegar used alone make an excellent dressing; the mixed herb vinegars also give an interesting flavor; lemint vinegar adds a fresh, cool, individual taste.

After selecting your vinegar, mix the dry ingredients, add to the vinegar, and bottle. When ready to serve a green salad, rub the bowl with a bruised clove of garlic, unless you are using garlic vinegar. Next break up your salad greens in the bowl, and pour over them enough olive oil to coat the leaves. Toss the leaves over and over, then sprinkle lightly with the mixture of herbs, condiments, and vinegar, and toss the leaves again.

HERB FRENCH SALAD DRESSING #2

For the cook who has no herb vinegar, common store vinegar may be substituted and the herb flavor added with the pulverized herb mix given in Chapter 3. Before making the salad, rub the bowl with a bruised clove of garlic.

HERB FRENCH SALAD DRESSING #3

For a variation, crush 1 ounce of blue or Roquefort cheese with a fork and add to the vinegar mix.

HERRING SALAD

4 luncheon herring (sold in glass jars, pickled in vinegar with spices)	herb vinegar
	2 teaspoons finely chopped chives
1 pound cooked beets	1 canned pimento pepper
6 medium-sized boiled potatoes	1 hard-boiled egg
3 apples	1 teaspoon tarragon
	1 sprig fresh dill

Cut the herring into small pieces. Dice the beets. Peel and cube potatoes. Peel and cube the apples. Mix all together with the chives and tarragon. Stir in about ¼ cup herb vinegar. Cut pimento pepper into narrow strips. Then chop the egg fine and strip dill from stem and cut up. Arrange herring salad on a serving dish and decorate with egg and pimento pepper.

Sprinkle with the dill. Chill in refrigerator and let marinate for at least 12 hours before serving.

PINEAPPLE ASPIC
Serve with Cold Ham

2 envelopes unflavored gelatine	2 cups boiling water
½ cup canned pineapple	1 sprig sweet cicely
1 cup pineapple juice	3 sprigs spearmint
2 teaspoons sugar	1 sprig lemon balm

Cut pineapple into small pieces. Strip leaves of herbs from stems, and cut up until minced. Dissolve the gelatine in cold pineapple juice. Add boiling water, sugar, herbs, and pineapple and pour into a chilled mold, and when cool, set in the refrigerator until aspic jells.

POTATO HERB SALAD

1 pound potatoes	⅓ cup chives
1 sprig young dill leaves	2 sprigs parsley
1 sprig sweet cicely	2 sprigs spearmint
2 sprigs lemon balm	4 tablespoons mayonnaise

Boil potatoes with jackets on in salted water until done, not overdone. Potatoes must be firm. Peel while still warm and slice. Cut up herb leaves, mix immediately with mayonnaise and potatoes, and chill in the refrigerator.

ROMAN SALAD

½ pound thin spaghetti	½ bunch carrots
3 leaves sweet cicely	1 can peas
1 sprig mint	mayonnaise, enough to blend in-
1 stalk celery	gredients

Cook spaghetti according to directions on package, and chop. Cook and dice carrots. Cut celery into small pieces. Strip leaves of sweet cicely and mint from stems and chop. Mix all ingredients with the mayonnaise. Chill.

SEAFOOD SALAD

left-over swordfish or halibut	10 cress leaves
½ cup peas (cooked)	10 lettuce leaves
½ cup carrots (cooked)	small young stalk of lovage
1 medium cucumber	3 tablespoons mayonnaise

Shred fish. Dice carrots and cucumber. Cut lovage in small pieces. Strip cress from stems. Break 4 lettuce leaves into small pieces. Mix all ingredients together except the remaining lettuce leaves. Place these leaves on serving dish. Serve salad on leaves. Chill in refrigerator about 10 minutes.

SUMMER LUNCHEON SALAD

¼ head chicory	3 sprigs salad burnet
¼ head escarolle	3 sprigs sweet cicely
1 green pepper	1 heart of celery or 3 stalks
¼ pound sliced salami	5 or 6 radishes
1 cucumber	

Wash and dry salad greens. Break up the leaves of the chicory and escarolle. Remove seeds and stem from pepper and slice thin. Slice radishes. Trim skin from edge of salami and cut into narrow strips. Peel and dice cucumbers. Chop celery. Strip leaves of sweet cicely and salad burnet from stems and cut up. Mix all ingredients in salad bowl with herb French dressing.

If you like more garlic flavor than the salami provides, rub the bowl with a bruised garlic clove.

THE VEGETABLE BIN

BAKED BEANS

1 pound dried pea beans	1½ ounces molasses
¼ pound lean salt pork	½ teaspoon marjoram
1 shallot	1 pinch thyme
1 teaspoon mustard flour	1 tablespoon sherry
½ teaspoon salt	

Wash and sort beans, and soak overnight. Drain, place in deep saucepan, cover with water, parboil over slow fire. Test by removing a few beans from the water and blowing on them. If the jackets crack open, the beans are ready for baking. Turn the beans and the water in which they were boiled into a bean pot. Score the salt pork almost through with cuts about an inch apart; bury the pork on the bottom of the pot. Also bury the shallot. Add the molasses, salt, mustard, and herbs, and enough water to reach to the throat of the bean pot. Bake in a very slow oven until done, adding water as needed. Time: at least 6 hours. During the last half hour, bring the pork and shallot to the surface to brown, and add sherry. Serve with dill pickles.

KIDNEY BEANS

2 cans (no. 2) dark red kidney beans
1 teaspoon sugar
1 finely chopped shallot

½ cup sherry
1 teaspoon mustard powder
¼ teaspoon summer savory
½ teaspoon salt

Bring the beans to a boil in the liquid from the cans, unless too dry. Then add a little water; add sugar, salt, and shallot. Boil 5 minutes. Add sherry, summer savory, mustard, and let come to a boil again. Serve. Especially good with meat balls.

MINT CARROTS

1 bunch carrots
1 teaspoon spearmint
¼ teaspoon sugar

⅛ cup sherry
salt and pepper to taste
1 tablespoon butter

Wash, scrape, and dice the carrots. Cover with water, add sugar, salt, and pepper. Boil until tender. Drain. Add sherry and heat. Then place in serving dish with butter. Roll carrots in butter, sprinkle with mint, and serve.

CREAMED KOHLRABI

4 kohlrabi
½ cup milk
2½ teaspoons flour
1 teaspoon tarragon vinegar

1 teaspoon celery
dab of butter
salt and pepper to taste

Strip outer skin from kohlrabi. Slice and boil in salted water until done. Blend milk with flour, then add about a tablespoon of kohlrabi water, vinegar, and celery, and salt and pepper to taste. Heat over fire, stirring constantly until sauce thickens.

OVEN BAKED ONIONS

8 medium-sized onions	paprika
¼ cup butter or oleomargarine	no salt
several sprigs parsley	

Peel and wash onions. Place in a pan with enough water to come about half way up the onions. Bake in medium oven until water is absorbed. Melt butter and pour over onions. Sprinkle with chopped parsley and paprika. Roll the onions in the butter. Return to oven for about another 10 minutes.

OVEN DILL POTATOES

16 small new potatoes	paprika
1 tablespoon finely chopped dill leaves or pulverized dill seeds	salt
½ cup butter or oleomargarine	fresh parsley or spearmint may be substituted for dill

Wash but do not peel potatoes. Parboil in slightly salted water. Do not overcook. Remove potatoes from water and place in a well-buttered casserole. Bake in oven, turning frequently with a fork until they are golden brown. Take casserole from oven, sprinkle potatoes with dill and paprika, add the remaining butter, and roll the potatoes over and over so that dill and paprika adhere. Replace casserole in oven until hot.

MASHED POTATOES WITH HERBS

4 potatoes	1 tablespoon chopped fresh chives
2 tablespoons butter or oleomargarine	salt and pepper to taste
¼ cup milk, or more	chopped spearmint leaves or parsley may be substituted for chives.

Boil potatoes, peel, and place in a bowl with butter, milk, salt, and pepper. Amount of milk needed depends upon size and mealiness of potatoes. Mash or beat lightly with an electric mixer while potatoes are still hot. Add chives, mix, and warm in oven.

RICE CASSEROLE

2 cups cooked rice	½ teaspoon parsley
4 strips bacon	1 teaspoon butter or oleomargarine
2 eggs	
1 cup milk	paprika
1 teaspoon lovage	salt and pepper to taste

Place rice in a buttered casserole. Lightly beat eggs. Add milk, lovage, parsley, salt, and pepper. Pour over rice and pat down with a spoon. Sprinkle generously with paprika, top with bacon and bake in a moderate oven.

THE SOUP TUREEN

HERB CONSOMMÉ
Garlic Croutons

4 cups beef stock	salt and pepper to taste
1 mushroom, fresh or dried	2 slices bread, cut in ¼-inch pieces
1 tablespoon sherry	
1 teaspoon lovage	1 clove garlic
1 teaspoon parsley	butter, oleomargarine, or chicken fat
1 teaspoon chives (chopped fresh or dried)	
1 pinch thyme	grated cheese

Cut mushroom into fine pieces, add it with the herbs and sherry to the beef stock. Boil about 5 minutes. Salt and pepper to taste. Strain.

Make the croutons as follows. Rub a cold frying pan with a bruised clove of garlic. Put in about 1 tablespoon of butter, oleomargarine, or chicken fat. Heat over medium fire until fat is hot. Then add the bread, stirring constantly and turning them with a fork until they are golden brown. Serve consommé with a sprinkle of grated cheese and the garlic croutons.

JELLIED CONSOMMÉ AUX FINES HERBES

1 cup cold beef stock	2 sprigs parsley
2 cups boiling hot beef stock	6 leaves mint
2 envelopes unflavored gelatine	4 sprigs salad burnet
3 small leaves lovage	3 leaves lemon balm
4 leaves cress	2 teaspoons sherry
2 leaves basil	1 teaspoon chopped chives

Cut the herb leaves very fine (aux fines herbes). Dissolve the gelatine in the cold beef stock. Mix in the herbs. Add sherry. Mix in the hot beef stock, add salt and pepper if necessary. Pour into a chilled mold, then let cool, and place in refrigerator until set.

Break up jelly into small squares. Serve in consommé cups.

MOCK BLACK SOUP

½ a calf's kidney	2 cloves
3 slices calf's or young beef liver	3 bayberry leaves or 1 bay leaf
6 beets	1 teaspoon parsley
2 apples	1 teaspoon lovage
½ pound prunes	⅓ teaspoon thyme
8 peppercorns	1 teaspoon sugar
¼ teaspoon ginger	2 teaspoons flour
1 cup sherry	salt
1 tablespoon tarragon vinegar	

Remove all fat and sinews from the kidney and wash. Mix ½ tablespoon salt with tarragon vinegar and enough water to cover kidney. Soak the kidney for 2 hours. Wash slices of liver and wipe. Peel apples and chop fine. Pit prunes and chop. Boil the beets separately in 2 quarts water. Remove beets and set aside for another meal. Use only the beet juice for this recipe. Crush the ginger and cloves and mix with other spices and herbs in the beet juice. Boil the liver and kidney in the beet juice about 10 minutes. Overboiling makes the meat tough.

Remove meat and put through a grinder, then return to soup. Mix flour with a little cold water and add. Bring soup to a simmer, add sherry, and serve.

MUSHROOM CUP

½ pound mushrooms
2½ cups water
1 boullion cube
¼ teaspoon black pepper
1 tablespoon fresh tarragon
    chopped fine

1 package unflavored gelatine
¼ teaspoon marjoram
2 teaspoons sherry
fresh parsley for garnish

Boil mushrooms slowly in water with the bouillon cube for about 15 minutes. Remove and discard mushrooms or use them for gravy. Let stock cool. Then re-heat 1½ cups stock and let come to a boil with the chopped tarragon, marjoram, pepper, and sherry. Remove from stove. Dissolve gelatine in ½ cup cold stock. Mix with hot stock. Let cool in a chilled mold. Place in refrigerator until jelly stiffens. Cube and serve cold in bouillon cups with parsley garnish.

THE CHEF'S ONION SOUP

1 onion
1 potato
⅓ teaspoon thyme
½ teaspoon parsley
3 grains cayenne pepper
grated cheese
1 tablespoon sherry

1 tablespoon flour
1 cup milk
3 cups beef stock or 2 beef cubes
    and 3 cups water
butter or oleomargarine
salt and pepper to taste

Cut onion into very thin slices. Peel potato and cut in small pieces, and boil in beef stock until soft. While the potatoes are boiling, sauté the onions in butter until golden brown. Blend flour in cold milk. When potato is done, crush it, and add to the stock. Add milk and sherry and herbs, cayenne pepper, and salt and pepper to taste. When onion is golden brown, pour stock into frying pan with onion. Serve hot with grated cheese.

YELLOW PEA SOUP

1 pound whole yellow peas
2 fresh ham hocks
½ teaspoon thyme
½ teaspoon basil

½ teaspoon mustard flour
2 sprigs fresh parsley cut fine
1 pinch pennyroyal
salt and pepper to taste

Soak peas overnight. Boil ham hocks in water until tender, about 2 hours. Add peas and herbs, salt, pepper, and mustard. Cook on top of stove until peas are done. A hambone may be substituted for fresh ham hocks. With a hambone, omit salt.

TOMATO SOUP AUX CROUTONS

1 can tomato juice (#2)	2 slices bread
½ teaspoon basil	2 pinches thyme
¼ teaspoon parsley	butter, oleomargarine, or chicken fat

Bring tomato juice to a boil in a saucepan, add basil and parsley. Let boil for a minute.

Sprinkle bread very sparingly with thyme. Then cut bread in ¼-inch cubes. Fry to golden brown, turning and stirring constantly to prevent burning.

Serve immediately with the tomato soup.

SPORTSMAN'S CORNER

BROOK TROUT

2 brook trout, half pound each	⅛ teaspoon thyme
2 teaspoons lemon juice	1 sprig fresh parsley
½ teaspoon tarragon	2 ounces butter or oleomargarine
¼ teaspoon rosemary	

Clean trout and remove fins, tail, and head if desired. Wash, wrap in paper towels to dry. Chop parsley. Melt the butter with the herbs and keep warm. Fry trout in butter in hot pan. When done, place on a platter, pour on herb butter, and serve.

GOOSE DU NORD

THE STUFFING

2 shallots or 1 onion	1 egg
2 apples	giblets
12 pitted prunes	½ teaspoon basil
5 slices bread	½ teaspoon sage
2 stalks celery	½ teaspoon lovage
2 sprigs fresh parsley	salt and pepper to taste

Boil the giblets until tender. Save the stock. Peel the apples, core, and dice. Chop celery and parsley. Put the giblets, shallots, apples, celery, and the prunes through meat grinder. Last, grind the bread to salvage juices in the grinder. Add the herbs and the egg. Mix well. Stuff the goose, making certain to leave a space of about an inch at the tail to allow for swelling. Sew or truss as with a fowl.

The Goose

1 wild Canadian (or domestic) goose with stuffing	1 teaspoon tarragon flour
giblet stock	salt and pepper to taste

Place the goose belly up in a deep roasting pan with the giblet stock and enough water to make about an inch in the pan. Preheat oven. Cook goose in hot oven for about an hour, turning the bird from back to belly, from belly to back every 15 minutes. Remove pan from oven, rub the goose with flour, salt, pepper, and tarragon. Return the bird to a medium oven and roast until tender, basting as needed.

The Gravy

liquid in roasting pan	1 teaspoon paprika
1 cup sour cream	1 teaspoon lovage
½ cup sherry	2 tablespoons butter or oleomargarine
1 shallot or 1 small onion	
¼ cup flour	salt and pepper to taste
2 teaspoons white sugar	

Heat butter in frying pan. Chop the shallot and sauté in butter until golden color. Add sugar, stirring constantly, until the sugar turns dark brown. Do not allow to burn. Stir in flour and lovage and when flour is light brown pour in sour cream and stock from goose pan. Stir constantly. Last, add the sherry, salt, pepper, and paprika. For a piquant flavor add 8 finely chopped green olives.

WILD DUCK

Stuff and roast a pair of mallards in the same manner as Goose du Nord (see recipe).

The Gravy

4 large olives, pitted	1 teaspoon white sugar
1 shallot or 1 small onion	1 teaspoon paprika
3 mushrooms	½ teaspoon thyme
½ cup sherry	½ teaspoon lovage
¼ cup flour	1 pinch sage
½ cup sour cream	1 pinch rosemary
1 cup duck stock from roasting pan	1 tablespoon butter or oleomargarine
3 tablespoons liquid from olive bottle	salt and pepper to taste

First prepare all the ingredients. Slice the olives, the shallots, and mushrooms. Mix the paprika and herbs together in a cup. Mix flour and sour cream together in another cup. Melt the butter in hot skillet. Stir in the sugar and continue stirring until the sugar is dark brown but not burned. Then pour in the duck stock with the shallots, mushrooms, and olives. Stir and bring to a boil. Mix in the herbs; salt and pepper to taste, and then add the flour and cream. Stir until the gravy thickens to the consistency you like. About a minute before serving, add sherry.

VENISON CUTLETS

4 venison cutlets	paprika
½ pound mushrooms	1 teaspoon summer savory
bread crumbs	½ teaspoon rosemary
2 tablespoons olive oil	1 tablespoon red wine
½ teaspoon sugar	1 tablespoon butter
cream	salt and pepper to taste
1 tablespoon flour	

Wipe cutlets. Melt butter, add the oil, dip cutlets. Rub in salt and pepper. Roll in bread crumbs. Sprinkle with herbs. Sear on both sides in hot frying pan. Serve rare with the following gravy.

Sauté mushrooms in hot venison juices. Remove mushrooms and place on dish with venison cutlets. Brown sugar in juices. Add paprika, salt and pepper to taste. Stir in flour and brown.

Add enough cream to make the required amount of gravy. Just before serving, add wine.

THE COCKTAIL HOUR: CANAPÉS

BROCCOLI OR CAULIFLOWER

1 fresh tight head broccoli or cauliflower
3 teaspoons mayonnaise
1 pinch mint
1 pinch summer savory
½ teaspoon parsley
1 teaspoon garlic vinegar

Cut the flower head of broccoli or cauliflower into small pieces. The rest of the head may be cooked as a vegetable. The sauce is made as follows.

Mix the mayonnaise and vinegar with the herbs and serve in a small dish set in the center of a larger plate. Arrange the broccoli or cauliflower on the plate.

CELERY

1 bunch celery
4 ounces cottage cheese
1 tablespoon sour cream
½ teaspoon paprika
6 small sprigs upland cress
2 young borage leaves
salt and pepper to taste

Wash and scrape celery. Cut stalks into 2-inch pieces. Chop cress and borage leaves. Mix the herbs, paprika, salt, and pepper, with the cottage cheese and sour cream until sauce is creamy. Fill celery pieces. Chill in refrigerator.

CUCUMBER

1 cucumber, not more than an inch in diameter
few slices bread
mayonnaise
¼ teaspoon dried marjoram

Do not peel the cucumber. Slice thin. Cut circles of bread with small whiskey glass. Spread each piece of bread with a dab of mayonnaise. Top each slice bread with a slice of cucumber and a sprinkle of marjoram.

EGGS HORS D'OEUVRE

½ dozen eggs
cream
½ teaspoon chervil
¼ teaspoon basil

1 pinch thyme
½ teaspoon mustard flour
paprika
salt and pepper to taste

Boil eggs in salted water until hard. (Salt in water will make shells come off easier.) Chill the eggs immediately and shell. Halve the eggs, remove the yolks, and place in a bowl with herbs, mustard, salt, and pepper. Mash well together with a fork and add enough cream to make right consistency. Fill the whites with the yolks. Sprinkle with paprika and garnish with chervil or parsley.

HERB BUTTER

bread slices
1 ounce butter

2 sprigs fresh mint or salad burnet or lovage

Let butter soften at room temperature. Do not melt. Strip leaves from mint stems. Cut leaves very fine, and blend well with butter. Cut bread in round pieces and spread the bread with herb butter.

HERB CHEESE

3 ounces cream cheese
3 teaspoons sherry
1 pinch sage
2 pinches summer savory

1 pinch pennyroyal
½ teaspoon paprika
bread slices

Mix ingredients together and serve on small squares or circles of bread.

SMOKED SALMON

¼ pound sliced smoked salmon
2 ounces heavy cream
2 teaspoons prepared horse-radish
½ teaspoon paprika

¼ teaspoon tarragon
⅛ teaspoon rosemary
bread slices or unsalted crackers

Beat cream until stiff with an electric mixer or egg beater. Then beat in the herbs and horse-radish until thick. Spread on small squares of bread or on crackers. Top with small pieces (1-inch squares) of salmon.

SARDINES

1 can small sardines in oil	¼ teaspoon tarragon
⅛ teaspoon rosemary	bread slices

Slice crusts off bread. Halve each slice, then cut each half slice in 3 parts. Bone sardines, and cut fish to size to fit on squares of bread. Sprinkle with tarragon and rosemary.

SHRIMP

1 pound uncooked shrimp	¼ cup mayonnaise
1 teaspoon salt	3 teaspoons finely chopped
1 teaspoon dill, or a sprig of	chives
fresh dill	3 teaspoons finely chopped pars-
1 teaspoon tarragon vinegar	ley
3 teaspoons prepared horse-radish	a few grains cayenne pepper

Boil the shrimp in salted water with dill and tarragon vinegar, about 15 minutes. Remove from stove and cool. Shell shrimp and remove small black veins. Store in refrigerator, in covered bowl to keep from drying out. Mix horse-radish, chives, mayonnaise, parsley, and cayenne pepper together. When ready to serve, fill a small dish with sauce, arrange the shrimp on a plate around the small dish. Pierce each shrimp with a toothpick.

PEAR OR PLUM TOMATOES

1 dozen small pear or plum	1 teaspoon basil
tomatoes	salt

Halve the tomatoes lengthwise, sprinkle with salt and basil. Serve cut side up. In summer, garnish with sprig of fresh basil.

PICKLES

BEETS

1 bunch beets	1 teaspoon celery seed
1 cup tarragon vinegar	¼ teaspoon pennyroyal
⅓ cup sherry	2 costmary leaves chopped fine
3 shallots or 1 onion, sliced thin	1 tablespoon white sugar
	salt and pepper to taste

Boil beets. Save one cup beet juice. Let beets cool. Then peel and slice thin. Cover with vinegar, sherry, and beet juice. Add shallots and herbs, sugar, salt, and pepper. Bring to a boil, and bottle immediately in sterilized jars.

BEETS
À la Maison

1 bunch beets	tarragon vinegar
2 shallots or 1 onion	¼ cup red wine
8 cloves	1 teaspoon sugar
1 tablespoon olive oil	1 small leaf costmary chopped fine
1 teaspoon young fennel stalk chopped fine or 1 teaspoon caraway seed	3 leaves peppermint, or spearmint, chopped fine

Boil beets in slightly salted water until done. Save ¼ cup beet juice. Let beets cool, peel and slice into a small deep bowl. Slice shallots and ring. Add olive oil and stir until beets and shallots are coated. Then add cloves, sugar, and herbs. Pour in wine and beet juice and enough vinegar to come just under the top layer of sliced beets. Weight down with a small saucer. Set in refrigerator and let marinate at least 4 hours. Serve cold. If too sour, add more sugar.

MUSHROOMS

1 pound mushroom buttons (small, unopened caps)	1 teaspoon pepper
½ cup white sugar	12 cloves
1 teaspoon salt	½ cup herb vinegar
	½ teaspoon marjoram

Cut stems of mushrooms level with cap and save stems for soup. Wash only if necessary. Spread on paper towels until dry. Place all ingredients in a skillet. Simmer slowly over a very low fire for about 10 minutes. Bottle mushrooms with juice while hot in a standard, sterilized preserving jar. Seal and place upside down until cool.

NASTURTIUM SEEDS

1 cup nasturtium seeds   white wine or grain vinegar
¼ cup salt

Pick the nasturtium seeds when immature, before they have hardened. If seeds are large, break apart. Soak overnight in enough salt and water brine to cover. Remove seeds from brine and cover seeds with boiling hot vinegar. While hot, bottle in sterilized jar and seal.

6

Growing Other Kitchen Herbs

'If a man want an Appetite to his Victualls, the smell of the Earth new turned up, by digging with a spade will produce it. . .'

William Coles, 1657.

ANYONE WHO has learned to grow the twenty-four basic kitchen herbs will have no difficulty in propagating other sweet herbs and potherbs, with certain exceptions due to climatic conditions. For example, because of its short growing season, sesame will mature and set seed only in the warmer regions unless it is started in a greenhouse. Conversely, people living in the warmest parts of the South find some herbs intolerant of the heat during the summer months. But most of the basic herbs and those in this chapter and the next will grow in a variety of climates. (See Appendix.)

Angelica (*Angelica Archangelica*)

HARDY BIENNIAL
SELF-SOWS
SUB-ZERO WINTERS

This tropical-looking sweet herb with large divided leaves and huge greenish-white flower umbels is a biennial, but one plant will grow for years if not permitted to flower. Angelica makes a

129

decorative background plant where rich, rather rank foliage and height are needed. It will attain a height of 4½ to 6 feet. Space plants 2 feet apart.

Angelica may be propagated by division of roots of second-year plants, but if allowed to set seed will self-sow freely. The plants like semi-shade and dampness.

ANNUAL

Anise (*Pimpinella Anisum*)   FROST-FREE MONTHS ONLY

This native sweet herb of the Mediterranean region is easily raised from seed sown during the beginning of the frost-free period. The plants grow to about 1½ to 2 feet high and bear umbels of tiny, whitish flowers and presently set the seeds used for culinary purposes. Thin to about three inches.

PERENNIAL

Bay, Sweet (*Laurus nobilis*)   SEMI-TROPICAL

This small, handsome, evergreen tree, native of the Mediterranean region, is most often seen in this country growing in a tub. Although one tree may attain a height as tall as an average tree, it lends itself well to trimming and is usually kept low, like a shrub.

The sweet bay tree is the historic laurel used to crown victors in the ancient Mediterranean world. It is also the bay that supplies the dried leaf used by the American housewife, the bay leaf. It is a beautiful, ornamental tree.

HARDY PERENNIAL

Bayberry (*Myrica pensylvanica*)   SUB-ZERO WINTERS

The handsome bayberry shrub grows wild in eastern United States, in sandy soil from Nova Scotia to Florida. It is commonly cultivated as a garden ornamental, prized both for the decorative grayish berries (fruits) that stay on the branches all winter and are used in making bayberry candles, and for the dark green, deciduous leaves that may be used as a substitute for the true bay.

This sweet herb attains a height up to 8 feet, but may be kept lower by trimming. For hedges, plant three feet apart. Set out shrubs in spring or fall, water regularly, and lime if soil is sour.

The leaves of this species are broader and the berries larger than those of *M. cerifera*.

Caraway (*Carum Carvi*)
ANNUAL OR BIENNIAL
SELF-SOWS
SUB-ZERO WINTERS

Caraway is easily grown from seed, and self-sows freely. The leaves of this sweet herb are delicate and finely cut, the flowers very small and borne in umbels that resemble those of Queen Anne's lace. The erect stems stand about 30 inches high, and plants should be thinned to about 8 inches.

Seed sown early in the spring will produce plants that set seed the following spring, in our garden.

Catnip (See Chapter 7)

Chicory (*Cichorium Intybus*)
Succory
HARDY PERENNIAL
SELF-SOWS
SUB-ZERO WINTERS

This European potherb and salad herb is tall (up to 6') with narrow green leaves. It is an escape in eastern United States, and is commonly seen growing along roadsides, admired by all for its exquisite light-blue flowers. It would probably be used more frequently in flower gardens if the flowers did not close about noon every day. Plant 6 inches apart.

Coriander (*Coriandrum sativum*) HARDY ANNUAL

The fruit (seeds) of coriander, sweetish and aromatic, prized by confectioners and cooks, are produced by a foul-smelling plant. Foul is the best word to describe the smell of the foliage, the flowers, and unripened 'seeds' of this valuable herb, one of the ingredients of Far Eastern curry. By this we mean that, though when ripe coriander has an interesting and delightful fragrance and flavor, the plants are not fit to grow in a flower or herb garden except in a remote corner because when the plants are immature, their 'fragrance' resembles that of the common stink bug often found in raspberry patches.

Oddly enough, this Oriental plant is hardy in a sub-zero climate. The 'seeds' germinate easily, grow very quickly to maturity, and should be thinned to about 2 inches apart. The quick growing plants attain a height of about 2 feet before flowering. The leaves are finely divided. The blossoms are white, in small umbels. Harvest the 'seeds' as soon as they harden and turn brown or they will fall.

Corn-salad (*Valerianella olitoria*)
Lamb's Lettuce, Fetticus   HARDY ANNUAL

This salad herb is easy to grow and has narrow, cupped leaves that are non-heading in most varieties. There is one variety that heads.

Sow in early spring, at same time as common lettuce, and plant again in late summer for a fall crop. Thin to 6 inches. The plant is called corn-salad probably because it grows freely in the corn fields of Europe where all kinds of grain are known as corn.

Fennel, Sweet; Finocchio
(*Foeniculum dulce*)   ANNUAL
Florence Fennel   FROST-FREE MONTHS ONLY

A Mediterranean sweet herb and potherb that is especially popular in America with Italian people. The leaf stalks of finocchio grow thick and wide, making an oval base. When blanched by banking up with earth, fennel is cooked as a vegetable.

Florence fennel grows from 2 to 4 feet high, with lacy green leaves and yellow flower umbels. It is easily grown from seed sown after danger of frost is past. Thin seedlings to 6 inches apart.

There is a perennial species of fennel, naturalized in some parts of America, that grows very tall.

Geranium, Rose (See Pelargonium)

Good King Henry (*Chenopodium*   HARDY PERENNIAL
     Bonus-Henricus)   SUB-ZERO WINTERS

This arrow-leafed potherb is an herbaceous perennial that dies to the roots with freezing weather. A rather weedy plant, the stalks grow up to 2 feet or more in height and the greenish, inconspicuous flowers are borne in spikes. The plants may be divided in early spring. Space about 10 inches apart.

                  HARDY PERENNIAL

Hop Vine (*Humulus Lupulus*)   SUB-ZERO WINTERS

This twining vine, a potherb indigenous both to Eurasia and North America, is well known for its use in brewing. It makes a handsome plant for an arbor. The large, rough, hairy, deeply lobed leaves grow thickly on shoots which attain the length of 10 yard sticks in one season. An attractive way to guide hop vines up the wall of a house to an arbor is to string three lengths of clothesline from a single nail in the wall at ground level, and spread the lines fanwise to the roof. In the fall when the foliage dies, cut off all the vines that have reached the arbor but leave a mass of twining dead brown stems around the ropes, to make a stouter rope for next year's growth. In mid-summer, the greenish pistillate (female) flowers begin to grow, and soon mature catkins, small green cones, hang overhead.

A hop vine is easy to grow from one small root. The plant is found wild in many localities and is a spreader. All but a few sprouts should be cut back drastically or pulled out.

                  HARDY PERENNIAL
                  SELF-SOWS

Horehound (*Marrubium vulgare*)   ZERO WINTERS

This hoary gray sweet herb is noteworthy for its foliage rather than its small whorls of white flowers. The wooly stems grow up to 3 feet high and the foliage is decorative. Space plants a foot apart.

Horehound may be raised from seed sown as early in spring as the hardy crops such as lettuce. Old plants will self-sow but sometimes are difficult to bring through a sub-zero winter. Unless covered with salt hay, old plants winterkill.

HARDY PERENNIAL

Horse-radish (*Armoracia rusticana*)   SUB-ZERO WINTERS

This coarse-leaved sweet herb has beautiful white flowers but is such a spreader that it is a nuisance in the herb garden. Find some unused corner outside the regular garden, plant root cuttings (horse-radish rarely sets seed) in a good, not too rich loam, feed with wood ashes and you will be rewarded with a crop of thick, white-fleshed roots in the fall, at which time the herb should be harvested. Set roots about a foot apart.

HARDY PERENNIAL
SELF-SOWS

Hyssop (*Hyssopus officinalis*)   SUB-ZERO WINTERS

This ancient sweet herb of the mint family is a sub-shrub which holds its leaves in northern climates well into winter. Easily propagated from cuttings, from division, or from seed, hyssop self-sows freely. Mature plants spaced about 10 inches apart make a decorative hedge about 2 feet high. After about 4 years, the old plants may become scraggly and should be replaced.

Hyssop leaves are small and oblong and green in color. The racemes of small bright-blue flowers bloom most of the summer.

There is also a white hyssop (*alba*), and a pink (*ruber*).

HARDY ANNUAL

Marigold, Pot (*Calendula officinalis*)   SELF-SOWS
Calendula   TEMPERATE ZONE

The pretty garden-flower annual calendula is the potherb, pot marigold. Easily raised from seed, pot marigold self-sows year after year. The stout plants with yellow to orange flowers grow about 2 feet high, and should be thinned to 3 inches.

Mints (Other than spearmint, for which see the basic twenty-four culinary herbs)

The true mints (genus *Mentha*) include a number of excellent sweet herbs in addition to the well-known spearmint. There is peppermint (*Mentha piperita*), which is one of the important industrial mints raised in large quantities in the Middle West and on the Pacific coast, and the important Japanese mint (*Mentha arvensis piperascens*). There is the beautiful gray, round-leaved, wooly mint (*Mentha rotundifolia*), sometimes called apple mint. There is curly mint (*Mentha spicata crispata*) and bergamot mint (*Mentha citrata*). All are hardy in sub-zero winters.

There is also English pennyroyal (*Mentha Pulegium*). (See pennyroyal under the basic twenty-four.)

Mustard (*Brassica japonica*)

HARDY PERENNIAL
SELF-SOWS
SUB-ZERO WINTERS

Mustard, close cousin of turnip and cabbage, is easily raised from seed and self-sows. The potherb often sold in the market for greens may be one of several species but the best for the home garden is that listed above. *Brassica nigra* is the black mustard commonly raised for making flour of the seeds. Thin to 6 inches.

Onion, Top (*Allium Cepa viviparum*) HARDY PERENNIAL
Egyptian onion SUB-ZERO WINTERS

One of the most fascinating of the true onions is the top onion that reproduces itself by means of a Medusa-like mass of bulblets, aerial bulbs that form on the top of the stem, and finally weight the stem to the ground and self-plant.

The fat hollow stalk, the flowering tops, the strange contorted growth of the aerial bulb all lend interest-value to this potherb.

Orach

Mountain Spinach: Green (*Atriplex*	HARDY ANNUAL
hortensis) Red (*Atriplex hortensis;*	SELF-SOWS
var. *atro-sanguinea*)	TEMPERATE ZONE

This hardy mountain potherb is easily raised from seed. The red variety is decorative, the color of the whole plant being deep dark purplish-red. Orach may grow as tall as a man. Thin to about 8 inches apart.

	HARDY ANNUAL
Pennyroyal, American (*Hedeoma*	SELF-SOWS
pulegioides)	TEMPERATE ZONE

The flavor of this hardy little American wild sweet herb so resembles that of English pennyroyal (a true mint) that the American colonists used it in the absence of the English species. American pennyroyal is an annual easily raised from seed and it self-sows freely. The aromatic plants are small and inconspicuous in the wild state but reach a height of about 14 inches and are many-branched under cultivation. Thin to 5 inches apart. (See Pennyroyal, under the basic twenty-four.)

Pelargonium (*Pelargonium*	
graveolens)	PERENNIAL
Rose Geranium	FROST-FREE MONTHS ONLY

This popular house plant is a sweet herb. Commonly called a geranium, the South African pelargonium is distinguished in several botanical details from a plant of the genus *Geranium,* notably in having an irregular flower. The flowers of the true rose pelargonium are purplish or pink in color. The succulent, much-branched stem of a pot-grown pelargonium may reach 3 or 4 feet in height, but good pelargonium culture should produce stocky plants with many flowers. Too much nitrogen produces unwanted 'leggy' growth.

The plants are extremely sensitive to cold and at the least warning of possible frost, they should be potted in good compost mixed with sandy loam, and placed in a sunny window inside the house for the winter months. There are many species and varieties of pelargoniums, very showy and fragrant.

Rocombole (*Allium scorodoprasum*)

HARDY PERENNIAL
SUB-ZERO WINTERS

This mild-flavored sweet herb sends up a spindly stalk that is soon topped by a small white bulb with a pointed tip that curves over in the manner of the head of a long-necked bird. The top bulb swells fat and round with a mass of tiny bulblets, aerial bulbs. Plant the bulblets 4 inches apart.

Roquette (*Eruca sativa*)
Rocket-Salad

HARDY ANNUAL

The leaves of this annual member of the mustard family resemble those of common radish. Native to southern Europe, roquette is found wild today in some parts of the United States, Canada, and Mexico. It is best sown early in the spring, or in mid-summer for a fall crop, because at these two seasons it is more certain to make the quick growth so necessary for tender leaves. This potherb requires rich soil and plenty of water. If cut back regularly new leaves will come.

Rhubarb (*Rheum Rhaponticum*)
Pie-Plant

HARDY PERENNIAL
SUB-ZERO WINTERS

The large, heart-shaped leaves of this potherb make a striking background for other plants. Rhubarb is usually propagated by division of roots. It needs a rich soil with good drainage. Buy root cuttings at a seed house, dig the ground deep, turn in a generous amount of compost, and then plant each root cutting at least 4 feet from its neighbor.

Always cut back the flowering stems to keep the plant vigorous.

Rue (*Ruta graveolens*)   HARDY PERENNIAL
Herb of Grace   SUB-ZERO WINTERS

This sweet herb and potherb is unpopular in modern gardens, because when handled, particularly on a very hot day, it may produce a skin irritation, similar to that of poison ivy. We have handled rue for years and have not experienced this inconvenience. The reports are numerous enough to prove that some people do react to contact with the leaves, which is unfortunate, for the plant is pretty. The aromatic, blue-green, divided leaves are borne on stems which are woody at the base and about 2 feet high. The bright-yellow flowers bloom in July and August in the colder parts of northern United States.

Safflower (*Carthamus tinctorius*)
False Saffron   HARDY ANNUAL

This thistly-leaved sweet herb is easy to grow from seed. The plants grow from 2 to 3 feet high and the effective yellow and red-orange flowers bloom in late July and early August. Thin to 3 inches.

                                               HARDY PERENNIAL
Saffron Crocus (*Crocus sativus*)   ZERO WINTERS

Saffron is an autumn-flowering sweet herb and a very valuable member of the iris family, indigenous to Asia Minor. The seeds take at least three years to produce flowering plants and it is best to propagate the nut-like corms. Plant them in spring or early summer, 4 inches deep and 3 inches apart. In September the lilac flower buds push from the ground. The orange-scarlet stigmas are the source of commercial saffron.

Renew the bed every second or third year. Dig the corms during the dormant period and replant the best and the healthy ones only. In cold northern climates, cover saffron crocus with salt hay after the ground freezes to assure wintering over.

Skirret (*Sium Sisarum*)

HARDY PERENNIAL
SUB-ZERO WINTERS

Skirret is an ancient potherb, now rarely propagated in this country, possibly because the culinary preparation takes time and patience. The roots, the edible part, are long narrow fingers, usually intertwined and of rather uniform thickness.

Skirret may be started from seed sown either in the spring or fall but, once established, the roots multiply fast enough each season to supply both the cook and also replacements in the garden. The plants live over the winter in cold northern climates and each spring grow into an ornamental hedge of green leaves 3 feet or more in height with small dainty compound umbels of white flowers.

If you plant the roots, leave about 8 inches between.

Samphire (*Crithmum maritimum*)
Sea Fennel

TENDER PERENNIAL
ZERO WINTERS

Samphire, a seaside potherb, is indigenous to the Mediterranean region and the shores of Western Europe and Great Britain, but it will grow inland. Sow the seed as soon as ripe, or propagate by root division in the spring, or take cuttings. The blue-green, fleshy stems and sparse blue-green leaves form a graceful plant. Set plants about a foot apart. Stems tend to be decumbent, and the plant is from a foot to 20 inches high. The cream-colored flowers are in compound umbels.

Because it grows naturally by the seaside, samphire requires salt. If you go to the shore bring back some rock weed for a mulch. Or, lacking a salt weed mulch, you can, if your sea fennel does poorly, dig in a half a teaspoon of table salt around the roots.

Savory, Winter (*Satureia montana*)

HARDY PERENNIAL
SELF-SOWS
SUB-ZERO WINTERS

Perennial savory is a sub-shrub about a foot high, with green narrow leaves, somewhat similar in appearance to hyssop but bushier, and with smaller leaves. Set plants 18 inches apart. Winter savory will self-sow, and may be propagated by cuttings or layering.

Sesame (*Sesamum indicum*)   ANNUAL
Bene   FROST-FREE MONTHS ONLY

Do not plant the seeds of sesame until the ground is warm. They will not germinate if you do. Sesame is essentially a warm-climate plant but if you start seeds in a greenhouse, plants will mature in the cold parts of the United States. Set seedlings 6 inches apart after all danger of frost is past.

The plants grow about 18 inches high. The flowers are lavender color and the seed pods are large. It is the seeds that yield the oil of sesame.

                                         HARDY PERENNIAL
Woodruff, Sweet (*Asperula odorata*)   SELF-SOWS
Waldmeister   SUB-ZERO WINTERS

Low-growing, sweet woodruff makes a pretty border plant no more than 6 or 8 inches high. The small, white star-like flowers bloom only in the spring but the whorls of light-green leaves make a decorative edging all summer long. Sweet woodruff self-sows or may be propagated by root division in the spring. Set plants 4 inches apart.

                                         HARDY PERENNIAL
Tansy (*Tanacetum vulgare*)   SUB-ZERO WINTERS

Tansy is commonly seen growing today along eastern roadsides. Many people think it is indigenous to America. This sweet herb was introduced to this country, however, by the colonists, who had many uses for it (see Chapter 4).

Tansy is so hardy that it thrives and multiplies in complete neglect, like a true wild flower, and is a natural spreader. We advise planting this escaped herb not in the herb garden but in some unused corner. The fern-like, strongly fragrant leaves are very decorative. So, too, are the buttonlike yellow flowers. The stems grow 4 feet high. Set plants at least a foot apart.

7

Ornamentals:

THE MEDICINAL, INDUSTRIAL,
AND SCENT HERBS

'For if delight may provoke men's labour, what greater delight is there than to behold the earth apparelled with plants—'

John Gerard of London, Master in Surgery, 1597.

THE MODERN GARDENER will find delight in growing some herbs as ornamentals only, either in the flower or herb garden, and many of the following species are very ornamental; some have fine bright flowers, more have interesting foliage, particularly for one who loves a gray garden. But, like the sweet herbs and the potherbs, they too were grown by Everyman, not for their beauty alone but for practical uses; for purposes as varied as making lip salves and antidotes for poisons; scent bags for the linen closet and charms for keeping witches from the door. To the modern grower, the word herb still has this fundamental meaning which is not the horticultural definition. According to Bailey, 'An herb is a plant that dies to the ground each year, or at least does not become woody.' And this definition excludes plants like lavender that to the herbalist are most certainly regarded as herbs.

Among the ornamentals, scent herbs, such as lavender, were used in the past for sweet bags, for potpourri (a jar of dried flower petals, usually with spices); for washing waters, for pomatums (cold creams), and some are still used today for the same purposes by the cosmetic houses.

Another important class of herbs, which includes many ornamentals, is the medicinal, valued by the ancients for making simples, home remedies. Some medicinal herbs are still used in preparations today sold by large drug houses. Still other ancient herbs were formerly used by cloth manufacturers for making dyes and some still are used for this purpose in modern industry.

Following is a list of medicinal, industrial, and scent herbs, all interesting, the majority ornamental, and many of them grown today by people in the cottage herb industry for making gift shop items such as sachets and toys for cats.

Aconite (*Aconitum Napellus*)   HARDY PERENNIAL
True Monkshood   ZERO WINTERS

This handsome, showy drug plant is often grown today as an ornamental flower for the back border. The true monkshood has erect stems 3 or 4 feet tall, and deep blue flowers. Known since ancient times as a medicinal herb, it is very poisonous. The roots were formerly used as an ingredient for rat poison. Obviously aconite should not be grown in the kitchen garden where some uninformed person might try it for culinary purposes. The poisonous alkaloid drug made from the roots is used as a heart sedative. The leaves are also used medicinally.

The plants are best propagated by root division in early spring. In sub-zero climates cover them with salt hay after the ground freezes. Space a foot apart.

Autumn Crocus (*Colchicum autumnale*)   HARDY PERENNIAL
Meadow Saffron, False Saffron   ZERO WINTERS

The meadow saffron is a very showy, autumn-blooming member of the lily family. The bulbs are large. Plant them, spring or fall, 6 inches apart. During the spring, very large and decorative leaves appear and, after a vigorous growth, die to the ground in July. In the fall, the beautiful purple or white flowers bloom.

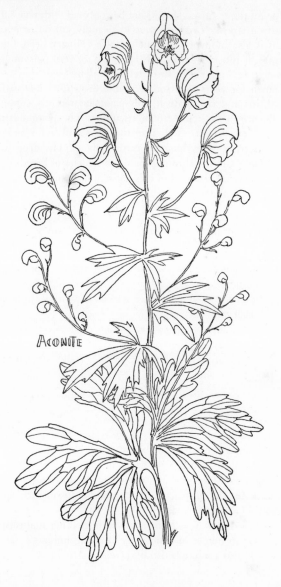

ACONITE

The meadow saffron should not be confused with true saffron or saffron crocus (*Crocus sativus*). Meadow saffron or autumn crocus is also fall-blooming but is not a culinary herb. On the contrary, it is a medicinal and the bulbs are very poisonous. As with aconite, keep out of the kitchen garden.

Known for years as a source of the drug used in treatment of arthritis and rheumatism, this plant has recently come into prominence in the science of horticulture. The poisonous alkaloid colchicine is extracted from the seeds and bulbs and used to treat seeds and seedlings of certain plants. The drug brings about changes in the chromosomes, the vehicles of heredity. Profound effects are reported in this entirely new and experimental field of horticulture.

Bachelor's Button (*Centaurea Cyanus*)
Cornflower

HARDY ANNUAL
SELF-SOWS
TEMPERATE ZONE

Bachelor's button, the popular annual flower, is an old medicinal herb. Dioscorides, the great Greek herbalist, recommended that the flowers be dried and used with salt to help the 'Asthmaticall, and melancholicall.'

Too well known to need description, cornflowers are easily raised from seed and will self-sow. Generally, the flowers are blue but some are white, pink, or purple. Stalks are 1 to 2 feet tall. Thin to 3 inches.

Bedstraw (*Galium verum*)

HARDY PERENNIAL
SUB-ZERO WINTERS

Yellow bedstraw is a rather spindly stemmed plant with a height of from 1 to 3 feet, the bright-yellow flowers and whorled leaves making it attractive on banks or in rock gardens. Easy to grow, bedstraw has been naturalized in the eastern part of the United States. To propagate, divide the clumps in early spring. Plant a foot apart.

Yellow bedstraw was formerly used in making mattresses. It is still used in homes in Europe for curdling milk.

There is also a white bedstraw (*Galium Mollugo*).

Bergamot, Red (*Monarda didyma*)
Bee Balm, Horsemint

HARDY PERENNIAL
SUB-ZERO WINTERS

Monarda didyma is the striking-looking, scarlet bergamot, much the handsomest of the bergamots. It is one of the few native American herbs commonly planted in herb gardens. The leaves are used as a medicinal tea and the oil is used to some extent in industry, but it should not be confused with the true bergamot made from citrus fruit, which is of much greater importance in the commercial world.

Red bergamot grows about 2 feet high and the flowers are flaming red, and of rather ragged form. Set plants a foot apart.

There is a white variety (*alba*). The species known as wild bergamot (*Monarda fistulosa*) has a purple flower and is commonly found on roadsides, blossoming in July.

Betony (*Stachys officinalis*)
Woundwort

HARDY PERENNIAL
SUB-ZERO WINTERS

This ancient medicinal herb grows 1 to 3 feet high with pear-shaped leaves and purple flowers in terminal spikes. It blossoms in cold climates during July. It is a hardy, herbaceous perennial, decorative in the flower garden. In the Middle Ages and Elizabethan times, it was an important medicinal herb. Writing in 1657, Coles recommended it for the eyes, the bladder, and the 'joynts.'

Betony can be propagated from seeds but seedlings grow slowly. It is advisable for the home gardener to buy plants. Set plants a foot apart.

Betony, Wooly (*Stachys lanata*)
Lamb's Ears, Wooly Woundwort

HARDY PERENNIAL
ZERO WINTERS

Although *S. officinalis* is the betony commonly used for medicinal purposes, wooly betony is included in most herb gardens, if only for its ornamental value. The nearly white foliage is decorative in places where low growth is needed. The leaves and decumbent stems are wooly and white-gray and the flowers

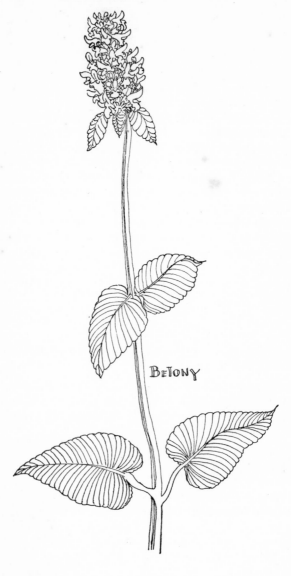

BeTony

are small and purple. Set plants 18 inches apart, and in an area where winter temperatures fall below zero, cover with salt hay after the ground freezes.

Bugloss, Italian (*Anchusa azurea*)   HARDY PERENNIAL
Anchusa   SUB-ZERO WINTERS

This medicinal herb from the Mediterranean region belongs to the borage family and, like borage, has rough hairy stems and leaves. The flowers in the true form are dark blue; in the Dropmore variety, purple. Plants grow about 3 feet tall and have to be staked. Bugloss may be raised from seed or old plants divided in the spring. Italian bugloss likes semi-shade. Set plants 18 inches apart.

The plant known as dyer's bugloss (*Alkanna tinctoria*) is also a member of the borage family but is not an anchusa. The root of dyer's bugloss, properly called alkanet, is made into a dye. There is also Viper's bugloss, a medicinal herb; and still another medicinal, common alkanet, which is really an anchusa (*officinalis*)! Like so many common names in the plant world, anchusa is confusing, but the *Anchusa azurea* is perhaps the best one for the general garden.

                                             HARDY PERENNIAL
Calamint (*Satureia alpina*)   SUB-ZERO WINTERS

This small member of the mint family is pretty in rock gardens. It grows up to a foot tall, with small purplish flowers in whorls. It may be raised from seed or propagated by cuttings or root division. Set plants a foot apart.

The aromatic leaves make a medicinal tea. Before the days of refrigeration, the leaves of this native of the Mediterranean region were laid on raw meat to 'recover' it, after the meat, in the words of William Coles, had become 'stinking.' Perhaps by this the author meant only ripe, our term for well-hung game.

Catnip (*Nepeta Cataria*)   HARDY PERENNIAL
Catmint   SUB-ZERO WINTERS

Catnip is a rather weedy perennial herb, easy to raise from seed, sown in spring or fall. If 2 or 3 well-grown plants are allowed to set seed they will self-sow and there will be more than enough seedlings to satisfy most gardeners, or their cats.

Catnip leaves are used as a medicinal tea but are of more importance to the cottage herb industry for making catnip toys. As John Gerard, writing in the year 1597, so aptly remarked— 'The latter herbarists do call it Herba Cattaria and Herba Catti, because the cats are very much delighted herewith—'

The leaves and budding flowers do delight cats, and catnip toys sell very well in the market.

The downy, heart-shaped leaves are green above, gray below; the flowers are purplish, and the stems are stout and grow up to 4 feet tall. Leave about 18 inches between seedlings.

Catnip, like most other important herbs, was introduced to America, but today is often seen growing 'wild' in abandoned barnyards, finding old manure piles much to its liking. It does best in soil rich in organic matter.

Chamomile (*Anthemis nobilis*)   HARDY PERENNIAL
Roman Chamomile, English Chamomile   SUB-ZERO WINTERS

This small, hardy Old World perennial with lace-like leaves makes a rather pretty border plant. The decumbent stems turn upward when in flower. Chamomile bears small, daisy-like flowers all summer long. The flower heads are composed of yellow discs and white rays, and are used as a medicinal tea for fevers and colds. The oil is a favorite hair rinse for people with blond hair.

True chamomile is easily raised from seed, or, if you have plants, they may be divided in the spring. Set plants at least 6 inches apart.

German chamomile (*Matricaria Chamomilla*) is similar but an annual.

ELECAMPANE

In folklore chamomile is known as the plant doctor. It is said that any plant set near chamomile will be made healthy.

Columbine (*Aquilegia vulgaris*)

HARDY PERENNIAL
SUB-ZERO WINTERS

This old medicinal herb of Europe, used in the past as a remedy for quinsy and believed by the ancients to have the power to keep dogs from barking at you, is now planted only for its beauty, but for that alone deserves a place in Everyman's garden. There are many species, and horticultural and named varieties of this popular flower, but the one most properly grown among herbs is common columbine (*Aquilegia vulgaris*) of Europe. Common columbine grows from 1½ to 2 feet high, with spurs about ¾ of an inch long. Set plants 10 inches apart.

The common columbine of America (*Aquilegia canadensis*) was brought originally from Europe. The yellowish flowers, with bright-red spurs, may be seen blossoming along Eastern and Mid-Western roadsides from May through July.

Columbine can be raised from seed but rarely breeds true. Roots may be divided in the spring.

Elecampane (*Inula Helenium*)

HARDY PERENNIAL
SUB-ZERO WINTERS

Most farmers who find elecampane growing in their corn-fields think that the plant is a native weed, unaware that it is an ancient medicinal herb from Europe. Elecampane has been naturalized in America.

Some varieties are short, some very tall and well over 3 feet, with tropical-looking foliage, and broad flowers, up to 4 inches in diameter, ranging in color from yellow to orange. This member of the *compositae* family is valued by the gardener who has a large garden with high walls. A good background plant which needs at least 2 feet of garden space.

In ancient times it was valued for more than its bold beauty. The thick roots have been used for centuries as a medicinal for heart and stomach trouble, and the leaves applied for sciatica. A specific recipe from Culpeper (England, 1653) calls for the 'fresh roots of elecampane preserved with sugar, or made into a syrup or conserve.' Roots thus prepared were 'very effectual to warm a cold windy stomach, or the pricking therein, and stitches in the spleen.'

For those who cannot find the ancient elecampane growing in their neighbor's cornfield, the plants are easily raised from seed. They also may be propagated by root division in the spring.

Feverfew (*Chrysanthemum Parthenium*)   HARDY PERENNIAL
Featherfew   SUB-ZERO WINTERS

This pretty plant has small, daisy-like flowers with yellow discs and white rays, and grows 1 to 3 feet high. It self-sows freely. Set plants 10 inches apart.

Feverfew is an ancient medicinal herb from Europe and the Caucasus region, used for centuries as a remedy for nervous headaches and neuralgia. For these aches, the flowers are steeped in hot water and served as a tea. A tea made of the whole plant is a homely remedy for fevers, and a tincture is applied to insect bites.

                                              HARDY BIENNIAL
                                              SELF-SOWS
Foxglove (*Digitalis purpurea*)   ZERO WINTERS

The Latin *digitalis* means 'finger of a glove,' and aptly describes the form of the beautiful flower of this herb, equally important medicinally to the ancients and to modern man.

There is little need for us to recommend foxglove, for it is so well known as an ornamental in the herbaceous border. The graceful stalks of the common foxglove bear racemes of bell-like flowers, purple in color, often spotted, and quite frequently white in cultivation. The height is 2 to 4 feet, and plants should be spaced 18 inches apart.

A common wild flower in England and on the continent, *Digitalis purpurea* is usually cultivated as a biennial although plants may live more than two years. Sow seeds in the spring or fall for next year's blossoms.

Fox Glove

Since ancient times the leaves of this beautiful herb have been harvested for making a drug important in the treatment of heart disease.

Fraxinella (*Dictamnus albus*)   HARDY PERENNIAL
Gas Plant   SUB-ZERO WINTERS

The name fraxinella comes from a Latin word meaning an ash tree, and this hardy perennial is so named from the resemblance of its leaves to those of an ash. The second and very appropriate name, gas plant, originated from the fact that the volatile oil from the flowers will ignite in a flash if a lighted match is held under a blossom on a hot, sultry night.

In addition to the plant's odd features, it is an old medicinal herb, the root being used as a remedy in fevers, and also it is a handsome, effective garden flower. Indigenous to northern China and southern Europe, the lemony, fragrant, dark glossy leaves and the equally fragrant large white flowers are very ornamental.

Gas plants are easy to grow from seed sown as soon as ripe in the fall but they will not flower until the third or fourth year. They may be propagated by root division, with difficulty, however. Once established, gas plants will grow 3 feet high and live for many years. Set plants 18 inches apart.

                                                          HARDY PERENNIAL
Germander (*Teucrium Chamaedrys*)   SUB-ZERO WINTERS

Germander makes an excellent low hedge for a flower border. The shrubby plants grow 1 to 2 feet high, and the small, crenate, shining dark green leaves are very attractive. The small but bright reddish-purple or rose flowers bloom in August.

Germander may be propagated from seed or by cuttings or root divisions in the spring. Space plants about a foot apart.

Germander was well known to the great Greek herbalist, Dioscorides. In the first century after Christ, he described it as growing in 'rough and rocky places,' and he said further, 'it must be gathered when great with seed; being newly taken, and soe sodden with water and given for a drink, it hath ye

power to help convulsions, ye cough, ye spleen having a schir-
rhus,—'

Gill-Over-the-Ground (*Nepeta hederacea*)   HARDY PERENNIAL
Ground Ivy, Ale-hoof   SUB-ZERO WINTERS

Gill-over-the-ground is an ancient medicinal tea herb, also
formerly used in the treatment of eye diseases of horses and
cows, and, before hops became popular, for making ale. Today
it is used as a ground cover in shady places where little else
will grow. It grows well under shade trees, and has to be ruth-
lessly pulled from the garden. Set plants a foot apart. The creeping stems grow rapidly, producing a mass of hairy, roundish
leaves that resemble in shape those of the common geranium.

Ground ivy has been naturalized from Europe in some parts
of America and is easily propagated from roots. The flowers
are small and blue.

                                    HARDY AND USUALLY BIENNIAL
                                    SELF-SOWS
Hollyhock (*Althea rosea*)   SUB-ZERO WINTERS

The hollyhock, native to China, is one of the oldest plants
cultivated by man. In Greece, Dioscorides wrote that hollyhocks
'annointed on with honey' were a remedy 'for ye stinging of
bees and waspes—' The flowers have been used for chest diseases.

The oldest form is the single rose pink, with some pure red
and some pure white among the plants seeded from rose pink.
The gay flowers are borne on tall stately stalks.

The strain we raise at Hemlock Hill is the old type and comes
from a few seeds we gathered one summer during a camping
trip in the Shenandoah Valley in Virginia. We found one,
seemingly dwarf but beautiful, single red hollyhock growing by
an old house foundation on an abandoned farm. The few seeds
we took from this one plant produced some red, some white,
and some pink hollyhocks. The plants of the first generation
were quite short. They self-sowed year after year, and each year
the plants grew taller until now we have hollyhocks nearly

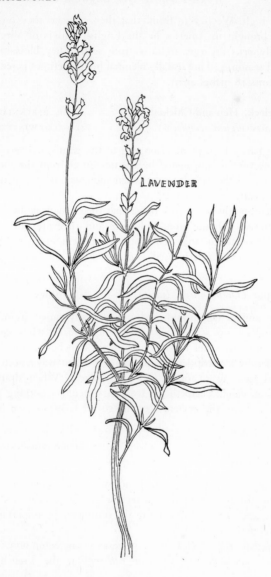

LAVENDER

9 feet high. We like to think that they grow as they used to when brought to America by the English settlers of Virginia.

Hollyhocks are easy to raise from seed. They blossom the second season, and are usually biennial but sometimes perennial. Set plants 18 inches apart.

Houseleek, Hen-and-Chickens   HARDY PERENNIAL
(*Sempervivum tectorum*)   SUB-ZERO WINTERS

The hardy rock plant belonging to the genus *Sempervivum* (live-forever) is propagated by rosettes offset from the mother plant, hence the popular name, hen-and-chickens. Set plants 6 inches apart.

In Europe there is a folk belief that these small, fleshy plants will protect a house from lightning and they are often seen growing on tile or thatched roofs. An ancient medicinal herb, houseleek was formerly used as a remedy for the shingles.

HARDY ANNUAL

Larkspur (*Delphinium Ajacis*)   SELF-SOWS

The annual delphinium larkspur is easily raised from seed and will self-sow. The deep blue, violet-blue, or white flowers come on stems about 1½ feet high. Plant 6 inches apart.

Called by Dioscorides, 'Delphinion,' larkspur was reported by him as growing 'in rough, and sunny places.' When 'drank in wine,' it would 'helpeth ye scorpion-bitten, as nothing else.' Others among the ancients recommended larkspur as a louse-wort.

HARDY PERENNIAL

English Lavender (*Lavandula vera*)   ZERO WINTERS

Lavender is a very important industrial herb. The flowers are used in the cottage herb industry for making sachets and pot-pourri, and in the production of the commercially important oil of lavender.

There are three well-known species: the one commonly called English lavender (*L. vera* or *officinalis*), the French (*L.*

Stoechas), and spike (*L. Spica*). English lavender has the finest fragrance and produces the best quality oil.

English lavender is difficult to grow from seed. The germination is poor and those seedlings that do come up, after an interminable length of time, grow very slowly. Fall seeding is often best but, better still, buy a plant or two from a nursery. Healthy plants are not difficult to establish if they are set in a protected, well-drained location. Lavender cannot stand wet feet. It needs lime. In a small garden it does particularly well against a stone wall. The lovely, misty, gray-green leaves look well all summer. The lavender flowers come in June and July.

A young lavender plant in flower will be about 18 inches high. A space of about 9 inches around one plant will be sufficient for several years. But year by year, old lavender plants spread. They grow bushy and wide and up to 3 feet high, and will need several feet of garden room.

When the plants are 4 or 5 years old they may be divided, or they may be propagated by cuttings.

In a climate where the ground freezes over in winter, it is best to cover lavender, particularly young plants, with salt hay. Without protection they sometimes winterkill.

Madonna Lily (*Lilium candidum*)   HARDY PERENNIAL
Annunciation Lily, Bourbon Lily   ZERO WINTERS

This ancient waxy white lily should be planted in Everyman's garden of herbs. The superb madonna lily was used centuries ago both as a medicinal herb and for making cosmetics. The great Greek herbalist, Dioscorides, wrote that 'Ye seed being drank is an antidot for ye bitings of serpents.' And the roots, 'Being beaten small with honey,—cleareth ye faces and makes them without wrinkles.' A very similar recipe was recorded in England over twelve hundred years later.

Madonna lilies are propagated from bulbs planted in August. The large (2–4 inches in diameter) yellowish-white bulbs bear leaves in the fall, and flower the following summer on stems 2 to 4 feet high. The madonna lily must have good drainage. Plant the bulbs with a little sand around them and in rich soil,

MADONNA
LILLY

8 inches apart. Well-rotted manure may be used and lime, as for most herbs, but no fresh manure. The madonna lily is one of the few lilies that likes limestone soil.

To the herb grower, the madonna is the important lily. There are a few other lilies, however, that belong in the herb garden, among them the scarlet Turk's cap (*Lilium chalcedonicum*) used formerly as a medicinal for the eyes and for childbirth ills; and the tiger lily (*Lilium tigrinum*). A tincture is made of the leaves and stems of the latter.

Like the madonna, the scarlet Turk's cap lily needs lime but lime is harmful to the tiger lily.

Moly (*See Ornamental Onions*)

Mugwort (*Artemisia vulgaris*)
HARDY PERENNIAL
SUB-ZERO WINTERS

We mention mugwort here both because it is an old medicinal herb closely related to wormwood, and because it is a nuisance in the garden. Mugwort is a rampant spreader, difficult to eradicate when once established. We raised some quite unintentionally. The plants came along with some other herbs from a nursery and we spent several years getting rid of mugwort. If anyone wants to raise it, we can safely say that they will have no difficulty.

Ornamental Onions
HARDY PERENNIAL

The broad-leaved moly (*Allium Moly*) is a pretty flowering onion with umbels of yellow flowers. Another very decorative onion is dwarf garlic (*Allium tuberosum*), a white-flowered variety. Both are hardy perennials. Space 6 inches apart.

Orris (*Iris florentina*)
HARDY PERENNIAL
SUB-ZERO WINTERS

The white-flowered orris is best planted in August or September. The fragrant rhizomes (bulb-like root-stocks) should be set about a foot and a half apart. The leaves grow about a foot to a foot and a half long. Orris is a European species, one of the

German iris. The rhizomes are sun-dried for the cosmetic industry—face powders, perfumes, and so on. In ancient times it was
commonly used medicinally for coughs, cholera, stomach-aches,
convulsions, and so on.

Peony (*Paeonia officinalis*)
HARDY PERENNIAL
SUB-ZERO WINTERS

The peony, recognized by most people today as a showy,
handsome garden flower, was, in past times, an important medicinal herb; the large fleshy seeds were used in the kitchen
and, in folklore, it was credited with power over witches and
devils. Dioscorides, the Greek herbalist, wrote: 'The herb Peony
is plucked up in ye heat of ye dog days before the rising of ye
sun and it is hanged about one and is good against poisons and
bewitchings and fears and devils and their assaults, and against
a fever that comes with shivering whether by night or by day—'

Indigenous to Europe and Asia, the red single peony is one
of the oldest forms. It grows 2 to 3 feet high and likes rich soil.

Peonies are propagated by division of the roots in fall. Make
sure there is an eye on each tuber, and plant a foot apart.

Primrose (*Primula veris*)
Cowslip
HARDY PERENNIAL
SUB-ZERO WINTERS

There are over 300 species of primroses indigenous to mountain regions in northern temperate climates of many parts of
the world; many from China, a few indigenous to America. The
herb primrose is a yellow-blossomed, old-fashioned flower, sometimes called cowslip, and native to Britain, northern Europe,
and Asia. The cowslip grows about 8 inches high, and is easily
propagated by root division. Plant about 10 inches apart.

The flowers are used for primrose wine. The ancients used
primrose leaves as a potherb, and the leaves and roots medicinally as an emetic.

DAMASK ROSE

Pyrethrum (*Chrysanthemum*
   cinerariaefolium)   HARDY PERENNIAL
Painted Daisy   SUB-ZERO WINTERS

This important industrial herb, used by gardeners in the form
of an insecticide, is the pretty, daisy-like pink flower known in
most old-fashioned gardens. One form of pyrethrum has white
flowers. The leaves have a silvery sheen.

Indigenous to Asia Minor, it was called pyrethrum by Dioscorides, the Greek word meaning 'much fire,' which described the
sharp taste of the roots. Pyrethrum is best propagated by root
division in the spring. Set plants about 6 inches apart. They
grow about 15 inches high. The flowers are the part used for
insecticides.

                                         HARDY PERENNIAL
Roses (*Rosa—*)   ZERO WINTERS

For centuries roses have been grown not only for their beauty
but for practical uses, for making rose water for hand washing,
for sachets and potpourris, for strewing on floors, for flavoring
in sweet dishes, and by the ancients for medicinal purposes. Rose
leaves with honey were said to drive away melancholy and to
strengthen the brain. Roses still are used for many of these
purposes, with the exception perhaps of the strewing and the
strengthening of the brain, and the herb gardener who wishes
to establish the best species for use as well as beauty, should turn
back to the old-fashioned kind. Too many of the modern
hybrids are bred solely for size and form of flowers. The scent
is often lost, although the fragrance of some of the new ones
is delightful. You may be sure of getting a strong fragrance
from the four roses listed below. The petals of the first three
and the leaves of the last are exquisitely fragrant. Set rose bushes
at least 3 feet apart.

Kazanlik (*Rosa damascena trigintipetala*)
Attar of Roses

This damask rose of semi-double form, with red or pink blossoms of thirty (*trigintipetala*) petals, is grown in the Balkans for the volatile oil distilled from the petals which is called Attar of Roses.

The kazanlik is very hardy and grows 3 to 4 feet high.

Apothecaries' Rose (*Rosa gallica*)

This is the ancient French rose used in the breeding of many modern hybrids. It is a single rose, dark pink in color, and the bushes grow to 3 feet high. The French rose in America will bloom in May or June, sometimes with a few fall flowers. Very hardy.

Cabbage Rose, Provence Rose (*Rosa centifolia*)

The cabbage rose is so called not for its size but for the form of the flower. The blossoms are quite small, light pink in color, and double. Whereas many of the old-fashioned flowers are single, the old Provence rose has always been known as a double.

Sweet-Briar (*Rosa Eglanteria*)
Eglantine

This rose is known for the fragrance of its foliage, particularly the young leaves. The pink flowers are borne in small clusters.

It is customary to confine sweet-briar in a wire enclosure, making a more or less circular mass of the foliage.

The roses mentioned above are cultivated in the same way as modern roses. They need good drainage, good rich soil, loam, or clay. They should be protected with a mulch the first season of planting.

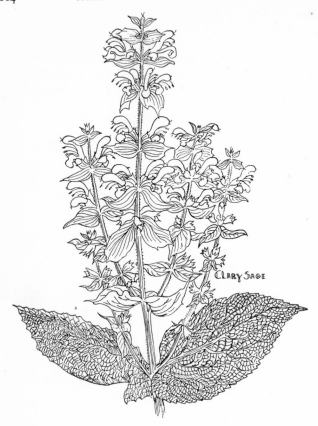

Clary Sage (*Salvia Sclarea*)

Clary is a beautiful sage, of rugged growth, which creates a curious, but, at the same time, striking and delicate effect when it flowers in the second year. A biennial, the first year there is a mat of large and broad (up to 9 inches long) hoary, gray-green leaves. The second spring the plant prepares to seed.

Great fat buds appear, like some strange green plant rockets. They grow upward on stout stems, taller and taller, until in June the stalks are 3 feet tall, bearing racemes of what at first glance appear to be quite large and very decorative flowers. Actually, the flowers are relatively small and it is the floral leaves, delicate bracts, that give a gossamer effect, particularly when the sun shines through them.

There is more than one variety of clary but one has pale lilac flowers, and whitish floral leaves tinged with faint green and lavender.

Clary is an herb to grow against a wall. It needs space, at least a square foot for each plant. Easily grown from seed in good garden soil, it will self-sow, and flowers may be had each season by planting every year.

Clary is an old potherb and today some people still use the leaves in the kitchen and for clary wine. Oil of Clary is a perfume fixative, and it was formerly used for eye diseases.

The English herbalist, Parkinson (1629), wrote of clary: 'The seede is used of some to be put in the corner of the eye, if any mote or other thing have happened into it—'

Santolina (Gray) (*Santolina incana, S. Chamaecyparissus*) HARDY PERENNIAL ZERO WINTERS

This fragrant, shrubby, small gray plant from the Mediterranean region is distinguished by many tiny club-like leaflets. Santolina makes a handsome gray border hedge from 1½ to 2 feet high. The button-like disc flowers are yellow and without rays. Santolina is best propagated by cuttings taken in the spring, or by layering. It is evergreen but needs winter cover in regions where the thermometer registers below zero.

Grown today mostly as an ornamental, this ancient medicinal herb was formerly used as a vermifuge and a moth repellent.

Southernwood (*Artemisia Abrotanum*) HARDY PERENNIAL Old Man SUB-ZERO WINTERS

Southernwood is an ancient medicinal artemisia closely related to wormwood. It has the beautiful silvery-gray foliage common to most artemisias, and is a good background plant, the feathery foliage reaching a height of about 3 feet. Space plants 18 inches apart.

The Greek herbalist Dioscorides reported, 'It grows much in Cappadocia, and Gallatia which is in Asia, and in Hierapolis which is in Syria.' It was then considered as an antidote for deadly poisons, and the seeds soaked in water and beaten were drunk with water for ruptures, convulsions, and sciatica.

It is often called old man because of its use in making a hair restorer.

There is a variety of southernwood with camphor-scented leaves.

Tansy, Fern-Leaved (*Tanacetum*   HARDY PERENNIAL
    vulgare, var. *crispum*)   SUB-ZERO WINTERS

Curly-leaved tansy has crisped, decorative leaves and is often grown as an ornamental. (See common tansy, Chapter 2.)

Thyme, Carpeting (*Thymus Serpyllum*   HARDY PERENNIAL
    and varieties)   SUB-ZERO WINTERS

There are many varieties of creeping thyme that will grow in soft, green or gray mats between bricks, flagstones, or field stones of a path or terrace. In return for being stepped on, they give off a most pleasing fragrance.

Carpeting thyme needs sun. It may be planted from seeds sprinkled between bricks or stones in early spring, or it may be propagated by root division. One well-grown plant may be divided into many parts which, if thrust into an open crack between two bricks or stones and watered regularly, will make new plants in a very short time.

The best-known carpeting thyme is commonly called mother of thyme or mountain thyme (*Thymus Serpyllum*). It has pale mauve flowers.

A variety with tiny leaves and tiny white flowers is classified botanically as *Thymus Serpyllum albus. Thymus Serpyllum coccineus* is a lovely, very tiny crimson flowering variety. *T. Serpyllum lanuginosus* has small wooly gray leaves.

GRAY
SANTOLINA

After flowering, the creeping thymes should be trimmed to cut away scraggly branches that tend to turn brown. Either snip off with garden shears or run the lawn mower over the path or terrace to promote a new and fresh growth. If given a little winter cover in cold climates, the leaves will stay green all winter.

Valerian (*Valeriana officinalis*)
Garden Heliotrope

HARDY PERENNIAL
SELF-SOWS
SUB-ZERO WINTERS

Valerian is easily raised from seed, and self-sows abundantly. The plants are tall, often 3 or 4 feet high, and should be spaced at least 18 inches apart. The pink flowers have a very heavy fragrance. Valerian makes a good plant for a back border.

The rhizomes are used medicinally, and the leaf is used to flavor tobacco.

Violet, Sweet (*Viola odorata*)

HARDY PERENNIAL
SUB-ZERO WINTERS

The sweet violet from the Old World usually has violet-colored flowers but sometimes they are white or rose. Candied violets are sometimes sold by confectioners, and the leaves are used for salads, and the petals are used for color in potpourri.

In ancient times, violet leaves 'being laid on,' were credited with helping a 'burning stomach, and ye inflammations of ye eyes.'

Large plants may be propagated by root division. Space plants a foot apart.

Woad (*Isatis tinctoria*)

HARDY BIENNIAL
SUB-ZERO WINTERS

The honorable woad deserves a place in an herb garden both for the stately beauty of the plant and for its historic importance in the weaver's trade. A biennial, needing good rich soil for proper growth, woad produces, the first season, a low mass of quite large, intensely blue-green, lance-shaped glaucose leaves. The following spring, strong blue-green stems rise up to 4 feet tall and bear in a panicle, a branching raceme of hundreds of small mustard-yellow flowers, the effect being a lacy, vase-shaped, golden spray, often 2 feet across. Five or 6 plants spaced quite close, about 6 inches apart, against a wall make a showy background of bloom in early summer. When the yellow petals fade the blossoms are succeeded by a display of dark, brownish seeds which, if they are not cut, will self-sow.

Woad leaves are particularly noteworthy, both for their fine color and for their importance in commerce. Today a dye made of woad leaves is used as a mordant for indigo, but before indigo was introduced to Europe from the Orient in the seventeenth century, woad was a truly important plant, both on the continent in France, Germany, and Italy, and in England. During the Middle Ages, woad growing was a lucrative business, subject to tax and regulation, for the woolen industry was dependent upon this ancient herb for the dye to color its wool blue. Woad was also used with certain dyes to make green and other colors.

The name Britain, so important in the history of the woolen industry, may even owe its origin to this dyer's herb. In ancient times, Caesar reported that the early inhabitants of England painted their skins with woad blue dye, and the word Britain is believed by some to have come from a Celtic word meaning 'painted.'

Wormwood (*Artemisia Absinthium*)   HARDY PERENNIAL
                                         SUB-ZERO WINTERS

There are several plants called wormwood but common wormwood is *absinthium,* the bitter herb that yields a volatile oil used in making absinthe and certain other liqueurs and appetizers, and certain medicines and liniments.

The foliage of wormwood is quite rank but if you have space against a wall, the gray-green lobed leaves and shrubby branches growing 2 to 4 feet high make an interesting background for plants with bright flowers. The flowers of wormwood are tiny and inconspicuous, greenish-yellow in color.

This hoary herbaceous perennial has been known in the Medi-

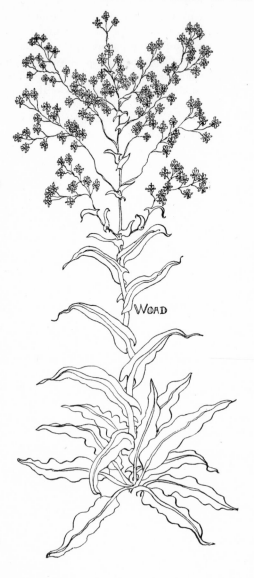

WOAD

terranean world for centuries as a medicinal, good for troubles with stomach and spleen, and also as a vermifuge. It is some-times found growing as an escape in America. Wormwood dies to the roots in fall. It is very hardy and quite a spreader, easily raised from cuttings or seeds. Space plants 18 inches apart.

Wormwood, Roman (*Artemisia pontica*) HARDY PERENNIAL
SUB-ZERO WINTERS

Roman wormwood has delicate feathery silver foliage. The plants grow from 1 to 4 feet high. Roman wormwood is used for the same purposes as common wormwood. It has been known since Dioscorides' time for making absinthe and as a moth repellent. In ancient times, it was recommended for heal-ing of 'Ye bitings of shrew mouse,' and the juices were believed to be good with wine for counteracting the effects of poison hemlock. Incidentally, poison hemlock is a biennial herb from the Mediterranean area and not the hemlock tree. Space 15 inches apart.

Yarrow (*Achillea Millefolium*) HARDY PERENNIAL
SUB-ZERO WINTERS

White yarrow, a medicinal herb, is a strongly fragrant wild flower common on our roadsides, indigenous to Europe, Asia, and America. It is too much of a spreader to bring into the garden but red yarrow, also known since ancient times as a medicinal herb, good for bladder troubles, ulcers, and so forth, makes a pretty garden flower. It grows up to 2½ feet high and is decorative both for the bright rosy flowers and for the many-cut (*millefolium*—thousand-leaved) grayish foliage. Space plants 10 inches apart.

8

The Cottage Herb Industry

'Camomill is put to diverse and sundry uses, both for pleasure and profit. . .'

John Parkinson, apothecary of London, and the King's herbalist, 1629.

THE HERB BUSINESS is an expanding market and bigger than many people realize. The mint crop alone is worth millions of dollars annually, and other herbs, indispensable for seasoning but neglected during the early days of the twentieth century, are again being talked of. Scarcely a day passes that we do not read in one of the nationally syndicated food columns in the papers or in a magazine article, about the revival of an herb known in everyday life to our great-grandparents. There is an herb society with a national membership; the public is becoming more and more herb conscious, and the cottage herb industry which began for us, as a hobby, may even become big business.

We shall take up, one by one, the phases of the herb industry which are most important commercially today, but first it is imperative that we give a word of general advice. One day after we had established our own cottage herb industry, the telephone rang and someone inquired, 'You have an herb farm?' To our affirmative reply, she said, 'Oh, good. I am coming right out to see you. We have a couple of old fields that are all run out and going to waste, and we thought we'd like to do something with them, you know, something easy, something that doesn't mean any work, and so naturally we thought of growing herbs!'

Old, run-out meadows could be made into a profitable herb farm but not by this person, nor by anyone else looking for an easy way to earn money. No matter how many people tell you that herbs are weeds, or that all you have to do is to stick a few seeds in the ground and reap the harvest, do not believe it. Because a few of the ancient medicinal herbs, for example, the plantain, flourish today as garden pests, this does not mean that commercially important herbs are raised without effort. The beds must be weeded, cultivated, and intelligently husbanded; insect pests and diseases must be watched for and eradicated; then comes the production and packaging which all means work, fascinating, pleasurable work, but work nevertheless.

The products of our herb garden that we have placed on the market are as follows:

CULINARY	OTHER PRODUCTS
Dried herbs	Herb and spice shelf
Herb vinegars	Catnip toy
Salad dressing	English lavender
Wine mustard	Herb plants
	Window boxes

Culinary Products

The simplest culinary herb products to market are dried herbs because no ingredients other than the herbs themselves are necessary, and very little equipment is needed in addition to that used in preparing a few jars for the home shelf. Quart Mason jars make good containers in which to store the pulverized herbs, the corn mill suggested in the harvest chapter is essential, and a large galvanized tub will serve as a place to wash the herbs out-of-doors with a garden hose. In order to drip herbs in any quantity, build a rack in the shade of trees or in a shed, with hardware cloth to cover the top framework, and, for drying the herbs, make five or six small screens (2′ x 3′) of hardware cloth, or one or two larger screens (3′ x 12′) with pulleys to hoist them to the ceiling of a drying room.

Making herb vinegars in quantities to sell requires more equipment than is used in the average kitchen, the most important requirement being containers large enough for marinating the herbs. For this purpose, we bought eight crocks, five- and ten-gallon capacity, with covers, the kind used on farms for salting pork and putting down eggs in water glass. Almost any farm supply house carries these crocks, and they can be used over and over again during the summer as the various herbs mature. The second requirement is a wholesale source of wine vinegar. We buy cider vinegar retail because we use very little of it, but the retail price of wine vinegars is prohibitive.

We bought our first wine vinegars from a wholesale grocer whose name we obtained from our local store, and the wholesaler delivered any amount to us over nineteen dollars' value. The second year we chanced upon what we thought was a 'good buy,' a barrel of supposedly four-year-old red wine vinegar owned by a friend of an Italian grocer in a neighboring city where we buy cheese. It had been intended for wine but had soured and the sample the grocer gave us was of excellent flavor, though not very sharp. We bought the barrel and our troubles began.

We received an order from a New York store and one day, some weeks later, we returned to the store, hoping for a re-order. The manager said they had sold all but one of our bottles, which he showed to us, and asked us what was wrong with it. Obviously, something was. At least a quarter of the vinegar was replaced with a strange translucent lump which was 'mother of vinegar.' Our 'good buy' of local 'aged' wine vinegar had not finished undergoing the acetous fermentation necessary to turn wine to vinegar. We replaced this bottle and filled the re-order with vinegar in which the acidity had been tested and was at least five per cent.

We mention this for two reasons. First, in the instances where something has been wrong with our products, we have immediately replaced them, and, by so doing, have retained the good will of our retailers who have never failed to give us a re-order. And, as to vinegar, unless you know a great deal about acetous fermentation, buy only what has been tested for acetic strength.

Even vinegar that has stopped fermentation needs endless filtering to make it clear. Storekeepers will not tolerate a cloudy product, at least in theory. Once we took a sample of our vinegar into a well-known New York gourmet shop and showed it to the manager. He held our bottle to the light, then shook his head. 'Too cloudy,' he said. 'Now here is the way vinegar should look.' He removed a well-known brand of herb vinegar from the shelf and held it upside down. To his obvious surprise, a dark cloud filtered through the liquid, which proves that even established firms have trouble with keeping herb vinegar as crystal shining clear as vinegar, of course, should be.

The essential equipment for producing an herb cheese salad dressing for the market includes one item, an electric mixer, which is a standard kitchen utensil today, and another item, a stainless steel bowl of at least 2-gallon capacity, which is not found in the average kitchen but may be purchased at a restaurant supply house. A mixing bowl of crockery will not stand up, enamel ware is unsatisfactory because it chips easily, and, as has been pointed out in the directions given for making herb vinegars, only utensils made of stainless steel, glass, or crockery should be used in making a product that contains vinegar. This means that all utensils, measuring cups, et cetera, for making salad dressing should be of one of these materials. Aluminum and iron, in particular, should be avoided.

The ingredients for a good dressing are not cheap but, as the manager of a famous gourmet shop told us, customers will pay any reasonable price for a high-quality food product. For our own dressing we charge $1.75 a pint, and this has not proved to be too high but even at this price we have to produce on a fairly low margin of profit, because we buy the finest quality, virgin-pressed (first pressing), imported olive oil. A dressing made with cottonseed or a similar salad oil will not sell in exclusive food specialty shops, the market for the cottage herb industry.

The condiments and other ingredients for making a salad dressing all, except for the cheese, may be purchased from the same grocery wholesale house that supplies wine vinegar. Cheeses are carried by wholesale cheese or meat distributers who will generally sell one cheese at a time at a substantial reduction from the retail price.

The herb French salad dressing in the recipe chapter is the basis for our formula, with the ingredients increased to make 4 dozen pints which, in order to assure a fresh supply, is generally all we make at one time. If the strength of the vinegar is five per cent, there will be no trouble with the oil in the dressing turning rancid, even during hot weather, but the principle behind delivering a fresh supply of any culinary product is that it is good business.

With prepared mustard, this policy of delivering frequently is absolutely necessary. Not that mustard will spoil, but after three months on a store's shelf, it will lose its bite even in winter, and even sooner during warm weather. The reason for this was explained to us by the wholesaler from whom we buy our mustard flour. The moment you mix mustard flour with any liquid, even water, a chemical reaction begins which gradually causes the preparation to lose strength. There is nothing that can be done to prevent this except to keep the jars under refrigeration, or to add an adulterant in the form of red hot pepper. But if the herb grower delivers a freshly mixed product, and not too many bottles at a time, the mustard should retain strength long enough for the turnover expected in the average store.

Packaging Culinary Products

Even if you sell only a few jars now and then, it is uneconomical to buy containers retail because it adds too much to production costs. Therefore, the first step is to locate a wholesale source of bottles and jars which does not mean a factory. In complete ignorance of the correct procedure, we started out to buy our first vinegar bottles by calling for an appointment at the office of a bottling manufacturing company which advertised in 'The Red Book,' the classified telephone directory of New York City. A short time later we were graciously received by a vice-president whose first question was, 'How many carloads do you expect to buy?'

When we explained our problem, he sent us to a jobber, who is the obvious person for producers at the cottage herb industry level, because a jobber will sell as small a quantity as a gross. And because there is almost no demand for odd lots of bottles in small communities, and as a result no jobber, to find one consult the classified telephone directory in a large city.

After the jobber has been found, the next step is to consider the size of containers. Pint bottles are popular for vinegars and salad dressing, although when the dollar is worth little in purchasing power, there is a greater demand for the half-pint containers. For dried herbs, the smaller the jars, the better, within reason. We first tried ¾-ounce jars but, because it takes so very little of each herb for seasoning, some of our jars stayed on the shelves until they lost their freshness. We now use ½-ounce jars for which we ask, and receive, the same price as for the larger size, and with a resultant increase in orders.

We have had a similar experience with mustard jars. Because few people use mustard every day, a big jar stays on the kitchen shelf until the product not only has lost its sharpness but also the neck of the jar has acquired an unattractive dark brown crust. A 6-ounce jar is big enough for prepared mustard, and if production warrants, use pottery, the standard bottling material for most imported French brands.

This brings up the matter of style and design which we have left until here, not because it is unimportant. Quite the contrary, a distinctive jar is extremely important; but when a person is in the market for only a gross or two at a time his choice is limited, and he is forced to compromise and take the best-looking containers of those available. Jars for mustard and dried herbs should be wide-mouthed while a narrow and long-necked bottle is more attractive for vinegars. The latter style should be avoided for a thick salad dressing because the solid ingredients tend to clog the neck of this type of container.

The owner of a cottage herb industry can make up with a distinctive label for whatever style the jars themselves may lack. The label should feature a trade-mark so individual that, by a glance, a customer can identify the product with the name of the firm. For a motif we chose an old silver caster, with vinegar and oil cruets and salt and pepper shakers, entwined with a wreath of basil, with two sprigs of borage beneath. Individual labels of this kind can be printed in small quantities, even as few as a thousand, at a nominal cost. The creation of the design, home-made in our case, would be an expensive item for most people, but this and the cost of the plate are necessary only once. From one plate, a printer can print the design on the labels, stationery, invoice sheets, and bill heads. We are not quoting figures on costs because prices change so rapidly that what we quote today might have no significance tomorrow. But we saved a little money on the first labels by having only our trade-mark and our brand name on the first 1000. On these we typed the name of each product and the ingredients in the space left blank. Incidentally, the law requires that all ingredients, and the total liquid measure or net weight be marked on a label of any food product sold on the market. As our production increased, we had new gummed labels printed with the name and ingredients of each product. These new labels look more professional, of course, but it is perfectly feasible to start with typed labels, especially in a local market.

After the first labels are printed, it is advisable to have your trade-mark registered. Write to the Register of Copyrights, Washington, D. C., and request the necessary papers which include instructions that are not too difficult to follow. You return the questionnaire with the fee—a nominal sum—and three of your printed labels. It is as simple as that.

The container and the label are certainly the most important items in packaging culinary herbs but as soon as we had our products on the New York market, we realized that they were at a disadvantage because all our competitors had display media. We therefore had a local woodworking firm make up a number of herb and spice shelves of the proper size to hold samples of our products. Three of our outlet stores liked the design so well that they ordered shelves for their own retail trade, and the small profit on them covered our initial expenses for our own display shelves.

Production of Non-Culinary Products

Our catnip toy was created during the early days of our herb farm. One morning we were sitting in our studio listening to the ominous pounding of the rain on the roof. I say ominous because it had been raining hard for days. The ground was muck, so that there was no chance to do any work in the garden, and our indoor work seemed as boggy as the soil.

'What can we make that will earn us a lot of money?' I asked my husband.

'How about something for cats? I read in the paper that one woman sold a million catnip mice in a year!'

'That just about floods the market with catnip mice.'

Silence. Thinking of nothing but cats, cats, catnip. What else but a mouse? Suddenly, listening to the rain on the roof, there came the obvious answer for a catnip toy. What was there for a cat better than a catnip mouse? A little catnip fish.

We made the design for a seersucker catfish filled with catnip and it has been carried by some of the big department stores as a leading item for cats. Incidentally, we advise anyone who creates a new toy of this kind to apply for a design patent at the Patent Office in Washington, D. C. It is not as easy to obtain a design patent as it is to obtain a copyright. We filled in the application correctly but the type of drawing required is very difficult for anyone to make except an artist specializing in patent work. We finally had ours done by an artist recommended by the patent office.

The reason for the success of this catnip toy is threefold: (1) we dry the catnip with the same care as we do our culinary herbs, and our catnip has an aroma that makes cats roll over and squirm in delight; (2) we make a rugged, durable toy that a cat can play with for months, sometimes even a year; (3) we harvest the catnip in flower but before the leaves fade, when, in a cat's opinion, it has the greatest fragrance.

At the time we designed this toy, we did not have enough catnip on our own place to supply the market, but our friends told us about some growing on near-by abandoned farms, which we gathered the first season. We already had the label, and it was a simple matter to cut out a rubber stamp from a rubber doorstop to print on the eyes and whiskers. For the seersucker we were referred by the office of a cotton mill to a jobber who quoted us a price by the bolt of 69 cents a yard. Not knowing

that, at the time, seersucker was selling for 99 cents a yard at
Macy's, I refused to pay the price. The manager followed me
to the street, protesting that he would lose on the deal, but that
we could have it at 63 cents. We bought three bolts.

A suitable box was difficult to find. We first tried in a neighboring city known for manufacturing hats and were told by
the hatbox makers that they would fill a minimum order of
five thousand. We had a similar experience in another town
with a factory for making boxes for alarm clocks, cartridges,
and so on, but we finally located a very small factory which just
happened to be discontinuing the manufacture of a pretty little
box of the size for our product. We bought 500 at a nickel each,
100 per cent less than any similar kind of box at retail. These
were the last boxes we used, because we found that the fragrance
of the catnip was lost all too soon in a cardboard container.
The essential oils were absorbed into the box. We now pack
our catfish in Cellophane envelopes and the freshness of the
catnip is retained well over a year.

For a display medium, we had the same box company make
up a standard box style used by bakeries, a display box big
enough to pack two dozen catfish per box. Our label and the
picture of a cat's head with a ribbon tied around the neck are
printed on the cover.

Having assembled our materials, we made arrangements for
several women to sew, stamp, stuff, and pack our toy in their
own homes, for slightly under a dollar a dozen. Thus, the more
pleasurable part, the growing and harvesting of the catnip, was
left to us.

Another popular gift shop item is lavender, which should be
harvested just before the flowers burst into full bloom. Do not
wash lavender, but otherwise dry the same way as culinary
herbs; when dry, strip the flowers from the stems and package
them in glass jars. Opaque containers are preferable because
they prevent fading, but they are more expensive. Needless to
say, the herb grower can package lavender in sachets of his
own design or make potpourri (pronounced po-poo-ree'), a
name derived from the French words, *pot* plus *pourrir* ('to
rot'), and refers to the old method of preserving flower scents

by packing flower petals in a partly dried state in a jar, layer for layer with salt. Fermentation takes place. Petals for pot-pourri may also be preserved dry, and marketed in glass or other jars, but flowers keep their fragrance longer if a fixative is added. Lavender flowers and rose petals retain their aroma the longest, but many other flowers may be used for potpourri, if only for color. The leaves of herbs such as lemon balm may be used also.

Another home herb product popular at herb fairs is a simple version of the pomander, a perforated, apple-shaped container of perfume mixed with white wax or other material and carried on the person to ward off infection. Some of the ancient pomanders were jeweled and very costly but herb lovers today often make pomanders of oranges stuck with cloves and rolled in various spices. The orange is allowed to dry, and then is hung to give a fragrance in a closet.

Marketing

The first question to be decided on before selling a single jar of dried herbs, a bottle of vinegar, or a catnip toy is whether to sell retail or wholesale. The following experience of a friend of ours will help you to decide which is for you. Recently we invited for Sunday luncheon the owner of a near-by herb nursery, who said that she had waited on a customer that morning before breakfast. Remember, it was Sunday, but customers come at strange hours to a store within the home. If you are the kind of person that does not mind keeping odd hours, if you can smile a welcome to talkative visitors around the clock and find relaxation in this kind of informal contact with the passing motorist, then the retail herb business is likely to be profitable for you.

The roadside stand is an obvious outlet for an herb grower with a house on a main highway, and even one who lives away from the black-top road may, with signs, lure customers to his place, for there are a surprisingly large number of people who will drive for miles to look an herb farm. It is fairly inex-pensive to set up a stand similar to those used for selling home-grown vegetables and fruits, or a room can be set aside in the

barn or house where products may be sold. This assumes, however, that the grower not only likes selling but also wants to
make a full-time business of herbs. But some people, like ourselves, have a profession, and have gone into the cottage herb
business as a part-time job. In our case, my husband, a mural
painter, and I, a writer, have no desire to substitute herbs for
paints and canvas and the typewriter. We want both, and so
we are carrying on a cottage herb farm as a half-time enterprise.
I think what success we have had is based on our decision to
keep our place strictly wholesale.

We sell to stores. Stores do not come to us to buy our products. We go to them and, within reason, at our convenience.
We are, therefore, masters of our own time. Of course in the
retail business you make more money for what you sell but,
on the other hand, you may spend a half hour selling one pot of
chives or a jar of dried mint for less than half a dollar gross
profit, and there is more bookkeeping. In the wholesale business,
even on the cottage level, you sell by the dozen, usually more,
and the invoice sent with the order is often the only bill needed,
with a follow-up statement on the first of the month if the bill
has not been paid.

Perhaps the most difficult part of the wholesale way, in the
cottage herb industry, is educating your friends and the manager
of the local inn to realize that you really mean it when you say
you do not sell retail. They cannot seem to understand why you
would not rather get $1.75 for one bottle of salad dressing than
wait for an order at $14.00 a dozen. It is the old bird-in-the-
hand philosophy that is hard to defeat. Not once but several
times we have had people ask to come out to our farm to buy
a sprig of fresh tarragon 'for tonight's fish,' and I have spent as
much time as thirty minutes on the telephone with a housewife
who wanted to buy a handful of dill for her pickles. Of course,
if we had a retail roadside stand or store in our house, we
would certainly sell bunches of green herbs, fresh cut, for there
must be a quite constant demand. But by insisting on no retail
sales, we have made the herb business what we intended it to
be, a fascinating relaxation from our professional work.

An obvious solution for running a retail herb business on a

farm where the owners have other occupations would be to hire full-time help, but if you have enough capital for that, then you are in rather big business and out of the cottage herb class. By cottage herb industry, we mean an enterprise in which the owners do a large part of, and perhaps all of, the work themselves. We hire labor only now and then.

We have made a successful arrangement with our local bookstore to act as a retail outlet for our town. A bookstore may seem an odd outlet for herbs and herb plants, but the owner of the store happens to be a friend of ours, his store is in a quaint colonial building on the village green, and herbs with their ancient lineage and literary background go well with books; our plants are on the front porch, and the culinary products indoors on an antiqued, maple-finish herb and spice shelf. We are thus protected from the motorists on vacation who like to spend an afternoon on an herb farm and go home with two bits worth of *Nepeta cataria* for their cat.

After you have decided whether to sell retail or wholesale, the second and very important step is to survey the market in order to study how your competitors are displaying their products. Do not copy, do something different. Also, note the retail prices in your district, for these are the basis for wholesale prices. Obviously, because of freight charges, the price in California cannot be the same there for items manufactured in New York and sold in the New York district and vice versa, but the price of an item marketed in one section would be about the same in the surrounding area. For example, when dried herbs are selling for fifty cents a jar retail in a New York gourmet shop, those on sale in New England should be approximately the same price.

In order to determine the wholesale price begin by discounting the percentage expected by the store. The discount on food stuffs is different from that of gift shop items such as sachets and catnip toys. We have found that our local dealer and most New York outlets are satisfied with 33⅓ per cent off the retail price on food products delivered to their door. For example, a dozen jars of dried herbs at fifty cents per jar, six dollars retail, would bring the cottage herb grower four dollars. In cases in which he does not deliver, he will have to allow a bigger discount. But in the toy market, no outlet will handle an item with less than forty per cent discount, and some want fifty.

We repeat, survey the market. Even more important than gathering information on prices and packaging, is interviewing managers of stores that you would like to see handle your products. Talk with as many as will see you, but be sure to make an appointment. The managers of stores are very busy people; if you telephone ahead, however, or write for an appointment, you will generally find them willing to see you and your samples, and to talk in some detail about the possibility of sales of your items. When we speak of stores we mean the gourmet and gift shops, which may include specialty shops within big department stores, but never the large chain stores. So long as you remain in the status of the cottage herb industry, you will not have the production facilities to compete with a manufacturer who sells by the carload and, therefore, you simply cannot compete with the suppliers of the chain stores.

Selling herb products wholesale at the cottage industry level has one decided drawback. We have found that no retail outlet within a hundred miles of our farm will give us a re-order unless we go to the shop in person. Time and again we have gone into a store carrying our catfish and been greeted with, 'Oh, we've been out of the catfish for weeks, and meant to re-order, but we knew you'd be in soon.'

The only stores that order by mail are those located geographically beyond our area, and, of course, this means we must spend hours on the road. A distributer, who serves a similar purpose in the food industry as does a jobber for the manufacturer of bottles, would eliminate our making deliveries and would get many more outlets because he would make it his business to call on shops from here to California. On the recommendation of the manager of a gourmet shop that handles our herbs, we talked with a distributer of fine honeys who wanted to expand his line and was interested in handling our herb food products on a national scale. His offer was very appealing but the first prerequisite was that we must be able to supply him in quantity, not by the dozen, not by the gross, but by the dozen gross. On this basis we talked prices in terms of 'mark-up,' or rather we tried to. The distributer demanded from us exact figures on cost of manufacturing salad dressing, and other products, and the smallest margin of profit we could, or would, take, and to that theoretical sum, he added his profit.

Quite obviously our figures, based on kitchen herb production, were unrealistic estimates. We were in no position to do 'mark-up' on a factory scale, and we quickly came to the conclusion that a distributer, though a necessity to a small manufacturer, is an unnecessary luxury to one still working at the cottage herb industry level—first you must have the factory.

We have made a compromise, however, with one of our products. The catfish is now being produced by a local business enterprise that specializes in manufacturing gift shop items. We supply the catnip, and they buy the other materials, oversee production and marketing, and we share the profits. This is a happy solution for the period between cottage herb industry and a factory of our own.

Promotion

While marketing our own products, several problems arose, among them the matter of exclusive rights. One of the first stores we contacted asked for exclusive rights on our catnip toy, and, believing that we would receive satisfactory promotion in return, we immediately granted the request. We soon regretted our haste. The manager did give us three lines in his fall catalogue, but no picture and no window display, although he explained that he was not to blame for the latter omission. The store cat that was supposed to hunt mice made off with every catfish sample the manager left in sight.

But even had this store given us adequate advertising, the sales from this single outlet would not have resulted in enough profit to us to keep the item on the market. Fortunately, the management gave us a release. The obvious conclusion is that when a store asks for exclusive rights they do so not to help the producer but to protect themselves from competition. A request of this kind usually means that the item is salable enough to assure a market for it in many stores.

As for advertising, the best ad for the cottage herb industry is a good product sold under an attractive label. Advertise occasionally in the home-town paper, try a small advertisement now and then in the trade papers, make up a colorful counter poster to give to the outlets, but, as the owner of one of the leading gourmet shops warned us, the small business person does not have the necessary capital to do enough advertising to have any effect, other than to lose all his profit. The owner of a small herb industry will gain more by depending upon indirect and unpaid advertising, often called publicity.

After we had placed our herb products in several metropolitan shops, we were advised to request an interview with a certain newspaper writer whose column on foods is internationally famous. With considerable trepidation we wrote her for an appointment which she granted us that same week. We came to the appointment with our salad dressing and catfish in our hands, not knowing just what to expect. The interview was very businesslike. The food editor looked at our products, and said she would try our dressing on a salad in the test kitchen. Meanwhile, she would have us photographed. We were hastened into the test kitchen where I removed my hat and coat and donned an apron; then we were presented with a salad bowl and fork and spoon and a head of lettuce. I assumed a look that I hoped was similar to one a gourmet would have when tossing a green salad, while my husband poured some of our dressing on the lettuce.

A few days later the write-up appeared and the publicity we received from this one interview brought us orders for salad dressing for at least nine months, not little orders but six cases (dozen) at a time. And the catfish sold too, because it so happened that the food expert had a cat who tested our catnip toy and approved.

We are telling this to show that if you have a good product you may get the most valuable kind of advertising without spending much money. Leave the paid advertising to big business.

Herb Nursery

Most important to the beginner in the cottage herb industry is the herb nursery because, while the grower is learning to know his raw materials during the years when she or he is experimenting with herb products, the sale of herb plants can bring extra income. The problems, however, of production and 'packaging' the actual plants are entirely different from those of the other herb products.

As the reader will observe, after glancing through the chapter on growing herbs, many herb plants can be increased by root division and while this entails work, the cost of replacement is relatively small. For example, if the gardener has a good, healthy, thrifty bed of tarragon, and sells a dozen or so big plants, he has but to pull off from each plant dug, a single, small shoot with a good root on it, set it in the hole where the plant was dug, and do likewise for each of the dozen plants sold, and he will have a dozen replacements. He can take one mature clump of lavender and, by root division, make a half a dozen or more plants, each of which will grow large enough to sell within a year.

Incidentally, although there is only a modest demand for many kind of herbs, there is practically a constant market for well-grown tarragon and lavender, and if the plants are large and strong, the gardener can name his own price. We are not speaking of the single stem seedlings one can buy in most commercial nurseries for under half a dollar each, tiny plants which will yield nothing to the buyer until the second or third year. We are speaking of big, hardy, field-grown clumps from which the buyer can expect a harvest the first season. For these tarragon and lavender plants the herb grower can get from a dollar to a dollar and a half in the present retail market, depending upon the size and age of the plant. Anyone who decides to go into the retail nursery business, however, must live at the farm all year around, and, in a cold climate, must also have at least a pit greenhouse for starting annuals and wintering over tender perennials such as rosemary.

We are listing here, in order of their popularity in our locality, the plants that in our experience are in most demand.

Tarragon	Basil
Lavender	Costmary
Rosemary	Mint
Thyme	Lemon balm
Sweet cicely	Sage
Origanum or marjoram	Chives

And 'Have you anything unusual, you know, some of those medicinal or strewing herbs?' For this kind of customer you have carte blanche. You can sell him anything, provided you use the botanical name and repeat a little of the fascinating folklore about the plant.

Plants for the market should be neatly potted. For retail orders common paper pots that can be bought at any greenhouse supply house, or even old berry baskets will do, but earthenware pots make a more attractive display. The latter are expensive but if used only for local sales, customers will usually remember to return them. For wholesale orders, wooden flats are best for delivery by car, and serviceable wooden tomato or other fruit boxes can usually be bought for a small sum from the local fruit merchant.

Window boxes planted with kitchen herbs make an attractive 'package.' Set on a porch in summer or in a sunny window during the winter months they supply sprigs of fresh herbs for salads and other dishes. Once we put on the market a window box of cypress wood with a stylized design in color stenciled on the sides but we had too many difficulties with these boxes which we shall relate in the hope of saving someone else from the same disappointment.

We arranged for a local woodworking company to make up fifty boxes for us on a profit-sharing basis; we were to give them half the net profit on the plants and they were to give us half of their profit on the boxes. For the plants we chose rosemary, spearmint, origanum, sage, salad burnet, and chives; all were herbs we had grown successfully in a window box on our own back porch. We had requests for tarragon but tarragon dies to the roots in the fall of the year and cannot be dug to make a new growth until after the ground is frozen, and we therefore considered it unsatisfactory for window boxes. For potting earth we used one-third sand, one-third garden loam, and one-third compost, well-mixed but not sifted. We set four herbs in each box.

Drainage was our first difficulty. Our original plan had been to have a metal tray inverted in the bottom of the wooden box but by the time the woodworkers had ordered the cypress, the price of lumber had increased and they could not afford to supply the metal tray. Reluctantly, we took the boxes as they were, and supplied drainage, as one does in a flower pot, with a layer of broken pieces of old clay pots. Then the real difficulties began. We planted two dozen of the boxes with our herbs and set them on our own back porch to give the plants time to root and look fresh. The plants soon recovered from transplanting but by that time several boards in the boxes had cracked, so that we could not market them. We set all our plants back in the ground, washed the soil from the boxes, and returned them to the company whose woodworkers were as mystified as we were to see that the cypress, the wood most often used in greenhouses for potting tables, and so forth, had split. After the company replaced the cracked boards and coated the boxes with a varnish that prevented further cracks, we again planted our herbs and finally delivered our orders to two big New York florists.

When, some three weeks later, we returned to see if the florists would place a re-order, we found that one store had sold half of the window boxes, the other store none, and the plants that remained looked as ill as some plants I once gave an overdose of 5–10–5 fertilizer. The reason was apparent. There was no sunlight in one shop, and not even daylight in the other, and the herbs did not thrive in the city air. To retain the good will of these two stores, we bought back, at cost, the boxes that remained which was three-quarters of the original delivery! Although this project was a failure for us from every point of view, we are convinced that the herb window box business could be a success, provided that the herb nursery has a greenhouse and a retail setup where both plants and boxes could be maintained and tested.

Registration as a Nursery

If you do try selling window boxes of herbs or even a single plant now and then, it will not be long before the problem will arise of shipping through the mails. The post-office clerk or the express agent will inform you that he cannot accept any shipment without a nursery inspection certificate which involves registering your garden as a nursery and learning the regulations governing interstate shipment of plant materials.

In our state, Connecticut, a nurseryman must register every year before 1 July with the state entomologist who has an office at the Connecticut Agricultural Experiment Station in New Haven. An herb grower must do this, even if he plans to sell only in his home town, provided that the state of Connecticut recognizes his herb farm as a nursery. In your opinion you may think you have a nursery, but you may find that your nursery is no nursery in the eyes of the state law which is not a reflection on your herb farm. You may be growing an acre or more of a certain herb and still not rate the name nursery. In our state, the name is reserved for an area where certain field-grown plants are raised.

To be specific, in Connecticut a nursery is defined as 'any place at which hardy trees, shrubs and vines shall be propagated or grown out of doors for commercial purposes.' Herbs such as lavender and winter savory, sub-shrubs, and the shrub bayberry come under this definition and other herbs that are 'Hardy herbaceous perennial plants may be subject to the same provisions.' Excluded are 'Florists' ordinary plants, unless woody and field grown.'

You can see that the wisest procedure before you sell a single plant is to contact the state entomologist. Then (once again we are speaking of Connecticut) the inspector will come and look over your stock. If your plants are 'apparently free from dangerously injurious insects and plant diseases,' the office will issue you a nursery inspection and registration certificate that will permit you to sell plants locally, and also interstate, again *if* federal quarantines are not involved.

A few of the herbs we raise at Hemlock Hill come under

federal quarantine for the gypsy moth, a serious pest which we
do not actually have on our farm, but which has been reported
in the surrounding area. We are subject, therefore, to federal
regulations on shipment of any kind of herb plant in which
the female gypsy moth may lay her eggs, namely, any persistent
woody-stemmed herbs such as bayberry, lavender, sage, and
winter savory. Of more difficulty to us is the Japanese beetle
quarantine. In very recent years, Japanese beetles have moved
into our area and all plant materials going from our herb farm
through the mails, by express, or freight, by truck, train, or
plane must bear both a state and federal inspection certificate,
if the plants are destined to points outside the regulated area.

There are several ways of treating plants to meet the requirements. Some nurseries commonly treat the soil in their growing
areas with D.D.T. or Chlordane. Some use other insecticides in
a dip or 'pour-on' method after the stock has been removed from
the field. In regard to possible use of these methods with herbs,
many herbs are grown for culinary purposes. So far no con-
clusive experiments have been made on the possible toxic effect
of D.D.T. used on herbs for the kitchen. Therefore, we do not
believe in using D.D.T. with herbs, nor at the present time do
we believe in dipping kitchen herbs in any chemicals although
the situation may change in the future. Horticulturists are now
working experimentally with dip and 'pour-on' methods that
may prove safe with culinary herbs.

Fortunately, there is a satisfactory method that involves no
chemicals and is safe and feasible for herb growers. In this
method the shipper washes all soil from the plants with water,
wraps them for shipment in soil-free sphagnum moss, or a
similar material, under the eye of the inspector who must be
present during the treatment. If, or rather, when you become
irritated by the regulations involved, all the red tape, remember
that it is for your protection too. While we who live in Connecticut are helping to keep Japanese beetles and gypsy moths
from entering areas free of these particular pests, in other areas
nurserymen and government men are working to prevent pests
now infesting other states from coming to Connecticut. By
working together with state and federal inspectors, we can help

control plant pests not only for others but for ourselves. Incidentally, you will find the state and federal inspectors not only most courteous and willing to go to endless trouble in helping you meet the required regulations, but you will also find them a source of information on pest control.

Therefore, as soon as you decide to start a commercial nursery, however small, the best course is to contact your state inspector and he will then tell you what regulations are in effect in the area in which you live. Regulations vary from state to state. Some states are exceedingly strict about incoming shipments of living plants, a few with regulations that amount to an embargo. To find the name and address of your state entomologist, contact your local county agent, your local farm bureau, your state agricultural college, or your state experiment station.

Herbs in Commerce

Anyone who grows herbs and has even considered starting a cottage herb industry quite naturally is interested in the future of herb growing in America. After the herb grower has expanded the home industry to the limit, what is the next step? There are many factors in the answer to this question, and the field is certainly not too well explored. In at least one herb industry, however, that of producing mint oil, the United States leads the world. Peppermint oil, one of the important volatile oils in commerce, valued in this country second only to turpentine, is in great demand for flavoring confections, dentifrices, and especially chewing gum, and it also has some use in medicinal preparations.

The commercial growing of peppermint, which started in the early nineteenth century in Massachusetts, has migrated westward, first to New York state, then on to Ohio and the fertile muck lands in certain parts of Indiana and Michigan where, according to the Bureau of Agricultural Economics in the state of Michigan, the value of the 1951 peppermint crop in that state alone was $1,390,000. In the early twentieth century, mint farming became important commercially on the west coast, in the states of Washington and Oregon, and the peppermint crop harvested in Oregon in the year 1951 was valued at over 3½ million dollars. Spearmint is also an important crop, and Japanese mint (*Mentha arvensis* var. *piperascens*) is valued for its high menthol content.

This brief outline of the history of this one herb industry illustrates the fact that herb growing can become very big business. Among other herbs grown commercially in this country are sage, caraway, and mustard (*Brassica nigra*) for flour, and during the last two world wars, there were experimental plantings in the United States of other herbs in commerce which will grow in this country. Information on the results of these experiments is incorporated in the Farmer's Bulletin, No. 1999, U. S. Department of Agriculture, *The Production of Drug and Condiment Plants*. The bulletin gives statistics on drug plants such as digitalis and castor beans, and culinary herbs from dill to dandelions. The advice to newcomers in the field, however, is all rather negative, with stress on the undeniable fact that producers here have difficulty in competing with the foreign market because of high labor costs at home. The mint industry has answered this problem to some extent with machinery which is a large initial expense, a mint still costing at the present time from $3000–$5000. But special machinery would no doubt solve the labor problem in commercial production of other herbs. Anyone who is particularly interested in scent herbs, the herbs of good smell, someone who likes to make sachets, potpourris, and pomanders should survey the market in the specialized industry of cosmetics and perfumes. While many of the commercial materials used are from animal secretions, for example musk, and some are chemical compounds, the perfume industry could not do without the essential oils distilled from the herb plants, which they have used for centuries. Roses, violets, and jasmine are important to the perfume industry, but of course the extraction of oils on a commercial scale is expensive, and it involves machinery for distilling or for other methods of extraction. Markets, soils, climatic conditions, and labor costs all must be studied, but this is entirely beyond the scope of this book.

But we do know from the survey we have made of the food market that herb food products have an unlimited field. Of course, the competition is stiff, as it is in any other industry. The producer must have not only skill but imagination, and the products must be superior in quality. A person who wishes to put on the market an herb sauce, an herb mustard, or a good herb salad dressing, will meet the same problems that confront anyone else entering this industry. But, particularly in this age when too many artificial ingredients are being used in foods, there is a market for good, new and non-synthetic products and seasonings.

9

Herbs Long Ago

'. . . he that would know the reason of the operation of the Herbs,
must look as high as the stars, . . .'

Nicholas Culpeper, From my House in Spitalfields,
next door to the Red Lion. 5 September 1652.

The Old World

ON MAUNDY THURSDAY, in the year of our Lord 1952,
Queen Elizabeth II of England, who had been Queen
but a few short weeks, took part in an ancient ceremony of the
Church of England, the distribution of specially minted silver
coins, the Maundy Money. The procession to Westminster Abbey
included the Beadle of the Abbey bearing the Mace, the Children of the Chapel Royal, the Choristers of Westminster Abbey,
and the Lord High Almoner and his assistants girt with white
towels, symbolic of the time long ago when the sovereign
washed the feet of the poor during the ceremony. At the end
of the procession marched the Queen's bodyguard of the Yeo-
men of the Guard in splendid traditional uniform.

When the Queen entered Westminster Abbey, she was immediately presented with a nosegay of sweet-smelling herbs and
spring flowers prepared by the Queen's herbalist: rosemary and
thyme, white stock, daffodils, primroses, and violets. Others
taking part in the ceremony received a similar bouquet. The
washing of the feet has been discontinued from the service but
the posy of protective herbs remains, a fragrant reminder of the
days when people believed that certain herbs had the power

to protect the bearer from infection, particularly from the dreaded scourge, the plague.

As we observe these same plants that are used in the ceremony of Maundy Thursday growing in our own modern garden, we are reminded of the historic importance of herbs. These and others set in prim Victorian dignity against a wall, or sprawling in weedy abandon, discarded by all but the true herb lover to neglect on the roadside, all have a mythical, brooding meaning in their green-gray leaves. When we take time to follow with our thoughts back into the world of our forebears, our machine-tooled intellects are startled perhaps by the provocative, often mystic symbolism in the familiar plant life that we know today for the aromatic flavor of its leaves and seeds, or for the ornamental effect that we are inclined to notice only as an accent in our herbaceous border; for many of our well-known flowers were formerly used as herbs.

When the first Queen Elizabeth was on the throne of England, herbs were used in many more ways than they are commonly used today. There were the protective herbs, such as rosemary and bay laurel, to ward off disease; there were the strewing herbs, such as rue, sweet woodruff, hyssop, mint, lavender, and again rosemary, which were forerunners of the modern chemical air refresher and were spread upon the floors to overcome the odors due to lack of sanitation. There was a long, long list of medicinal herbs, prepared with other herb products such as washing waters and perfumes in a special room called the Still-Room, set aside for the purpose.

A twentieth-century physician is no less dependent upon plant life for many of his drugs than was the doctor of old. The following are a few sources of modern drugs: the cinchona tree, source of quinine used in the treatment of malaria; *Atropa belladonna,* commonly called deadly nightshade, source of medicine used in treatment of eye disorders; and that indispensable, powerful heart stimulant, digitalis, the plant known to every flower gardener as common foxglove. The modern physician, however, orders medicines in a prepared form from a drug store, whereas in earlier times the physician often 'grew' his own drugs.

The garden of John Gerard, master in surgery and Elizabethan author, contained at one time over 1000 different plants. Shakespeare probably knew Gerard's garden.

There's rosemary, that's for remembrance; pray, love, remember:

These often-quoted lines spoken by Ophelia in *Hamlet* are but one instance of innumerable references to herbs in Shakespeare's plays.

A remedy by John Gerard, recorded in the old English herbal written by him, calls for the flowers of 'Lavender picked from the knaps, I meane the blew part, and not the husks,' he explains. This is, of course, the lavender we raise for use in sachets and potpourri. In Gerard's recipe the flowers were 'mixed with cinamon, nutmegs, and cloves,' and 'made into a powder, and given to drinke in the distilled water thereof.' This prescription, so Gerard claimed, was good for 'the panting and passion of the hart,' and prevailed 'against giddinesse, turning or swimming of the braine, and members subject to the palsie.'

Contemporaries of Gerard accused him of plagiarism but however he may have gotten his material, we today feel grateful to him for preserving for us in a printed form so much of the rich old herb-lore, the *materia medica* of the Shakespearean world.

An historic form of herb garden, the knot garden, was popular in Elizabethan days. It was a geometric pattern laid out with herb plants, within a square confined by boards, tiles, or other materials. Although to people accustomed to the simplicity of modern design, knot gardens may seem too elaborate, many of them were lovely in form.

William Lawson, who wrote the first gardening book published in English for women in 1617, lists the garden forms as 'Cinkfoil, Flower-de-luce, the Tre-foy, the Fret, the Lozenge, Cross-Bow, Diamond—' all living geometric plant arrangements. The santolinas and germander lend themselves to knot forms. Those mentioned by Lawson as 'comely and durable for squares and knots—' include roses, rosemary, lavender, bee flowers, 'Isop' (hyssop), sage, 'time,' cowslips (yellow primroses), 'piony,' daisies, pinks, southernwood, and lilies.

Knot gardens were commonly raised above the level of the ground because as that good gardener Lawson so aptly pointed out, herbs 'can neither abide moisture nor drought in such excessive measure as trees;—and this is the cause—that gardeners raise their squares—'

There were periods when geometric gardens were woefully artificial and garish, materials other than plants being unwisely employed. Bacon made a classic protest against the 'making of Knots and Figures, with divers Colored Earths.' He declared, 'they be but toys, you may see as good sights many times in Tarts. . .' But modern gardeners who confine their designs to the plants themselves can produce interesting formal arrangements that are pleasing to the eye, and examples of traditional designs may be studied today in America in botanical gardens. Some of these feature knot gardens, others the parterre (a later geometric form, with no artificial confining borders, and a more or less embroidered effect on ground level). Also, one can find examples of a medieval garden court, Shakespearean and Biblical gardens, and the medicinal. (See Appendix.)

Bees delight in the flowers of thyme and many other herbs, and bee hives have long been associated with herb gardens. The traditional form of the skep of twisted straw is an ornament for a modern garden, even if the owner does not keep bees. Formerly, honey was used by Everyman for sweetening, and in England even today a kind of mead is made commercially of honey and herbs, after an old recipe.

Sundials are also traditional in the herb garden.

If the great Elizabethan herbalist, Gerard, did borrow freely, or some say copy, word for word another man's manuscript, all of the early English herbalists to a certain extent borrowed, especially from the great Greek herbalist of the first century of the Christian era, Dioscorides of Anazarba in Cilicia. The Greek Herbal was not printed in English until the twentieth century, nor was it even 'Englished' until the middle of the seventeenth century. The manuscript, however, was known to scholars. The Greek Herbal is a large work, containing information on the use of hundreds of aromatics, roots, juices, wines, and so on; it contains the names of some unknown herbs and some others that are very common today, such as parsley which, without even thinking of it as an herb, everyone uses as garnish or in parsley soup. Dioscorides recommended parsley as a medicinal. 'Parsley grows in rockie, and mountainous places— Both ye seed and ye root hath an ureticall faculty being drank in wine,' says Dioscorides. The grammar and spelling are those of the scholar John Goodyear, who 'Englished' the Greek Herbal in 1655.

Certainly some of the material in the Greek Herbal surprised us. In the days before we discovered the Oxford University Press English edition of Dioscorides (edited by Robert T. Gunther, 1933), we believed that certain herb folklore familiar to us was of relatively recent origin, certainly not many centuries old. For example, take the use of pennyroyal, pronounced pennyry'al by old-fashioned folk. From our grandmothers we had heard that this old wives' tea herb was medicinal, that it would cure indigestion, and from our own personal experience, we proved the effectiveness of this old herbal remedy which we tried during a bad session of upset stomach. The results were so effective that now when we have digestive troubles, the first thing we do is brew some 'pennyry'al' tea from plants we grow in our own herb garden. Imagine our delight in meeting pennyroyal in Dioscorides, and furthermore to read that pennyroyal 'assuageth ye nauseousness and gnawings of ye stomach.' And Dioscorides believed that pennyroyal would do much more than that. The Greek claimed, 'it is good for ye gouty being laid on till the appearance of redness.' For this we cannot vouch, nor have we tested a third Dioscoridian treatment—'being drank with wine, it helps ye bitten of serpents.' But we do agree that pennyroyal 'assuageth ye nauseousness and gnawings of ye stomach,' today as it did nineteen hundred years ago.

Startling as it is to think that this homely and effective herbal remedy of our own grandmothers' time has been handed down to us through all these centuries, we are also startled to read some of the other Greek cures. These include drugs concocted from living creatures, such *materia medica* as the ashes of Sea-Horse, the ashes of River Crabs, 'rosted' or raw, earthly Scorpions, gall of Sea Scorpion, the flesh of the Viper, the Slough of Snakes, the roasted 'braine' of a Land Hare, the stones of the Hippopotamus, a broth of frogs in 'salt and oyle,' the burnt skin of the Earth Hedgehog, the dried 'lunges of a Fox,' an ass's Liver, Spavins of Horses, the Liver of a Mad Dog, and the scrapings of Elephant's tooth.

But if these medicinal ingredients seem strange to us today, if some of the ancient writers seem almost as 'mad' as Shake-speare's Ophelia, we must remember that we too live in a strange era. While Dioscorides prescribed the flesh of the viper, our physicians prescribe molds such as penicillin, and all sorts of weird injections, including blood from our fellow men.

Also when we read the scholarly Dioscorides Herbal and other ancient books, we must not forget one factor; that the world was then inhabited by many kinds of beings that few people will admit the existence of today. Not only was Dios-corides' world crawling with real, venomous snakes and beasts and poisonous scorpions (for whose 'bitings' he had herbal remedies), but it was also peopled with very real witches and devils, about whom he also had good advice. 'If any have ye herb Artemisia with him—it disolves weariness, and he that bears it on his feet, drives away venemous beasts and devils.' The Artemisia that Dioscorides recommends as an amulet against weariness and devils is thought by authorities to be mugwort, which, unless a gardener be very much troubled with devils, had best be left out of the garden, for mugwort (*Artemisia vulgaris*) has a way of traveling underground and spreading so rapidly that the average gardener is both wearied and bedeviled trying to get rid of it.

But before the twentieth century common man could not buy such miracle drugs as the antibiotics, or such strange protective medicines as the antihistamines, or such a wonderful antidote 'against giddinesse, turning or swimming of the braine' as modern aspirin. The drug store of yesterday was a man's garden, and man had to make his own medicines, and those who could not read Greek or any other language depended upon recipes handed down to them from their ancestors. Many of these old recipes were proved by trial and error by any number of gen-erations, and certainly the ingredients of some are worthy of study by modern chemists. If, now and then, there was a bit of witchery included, perhaps it was not too different from the modern psychosomatic approach to patients.

Aside from purely medical remedies, the housewife cherished other recipes handed down to her from her mother who in turn had them from her mother and so on back for hundreds of years, even before the time when the Western world had been converted to Christianity. Besides remedies for gout, the itch, stomach-ache, and the myriad of common ills man had then as now, the housewife knew how to make her own cosmetics, her lip salve, her rouge, and preventatives of that dreadful bogey, growing old.

Today we can learn some of these old recipes in *The Toilet of Flora,* anonymous, a book printed in London for J. Murray, No. 32, Fleet Street, and W. Nicoll, St. Paul's Church Yard, in 1779. *The Toilet of Flora* contains 'Receipts for Cosmetics of every kind, that can smooth and brighten the Skin, give Force to Beauty, and take off the Appearance of Old Age and Decay.' In addition to instructions for making lip salves and fine perfumes, there is a formula for dyeing the hair or beard black, one for curing corns on the feet, another approved for use against that troublesome complaint, 'Teeth set on Edge,' and also certain methods of destroying fleas, and so forth. We shall quote only two.

One for the ladies:

'A Pomatum [cold cream] for Wrinkles.

'Take juice of White Lily Roots and fine Honey, of each two ounces; melted white wax, an ounce; incorporate the whole together, and make a pomatum. It should be applied every night, and not be wiped off till the next morning.'

The White Lily called for in the recipe, and the one commonly used as an herb in ancient times, is the handsome garden lily, *Lilium candidum,* the madonna.

And if ladies have been troubled through history with wrinkles, we have help also for a trouble commonly experienced only by men.

'A Compound Oil to quicken the Growth of Hair.

'Take a half a pound of green Southernwood bruised, boil

it in a pint and a half of Sweet Oil, and a half a pint of Red Wine; when sufficient boiled, remove it from the fire, and strain off the liquor through a linen bag; repeat this operation three times with fresh Southernwood. The last time add to the strained liquor two ounces of Bears-grease.

'This oil quickly makes the hair shoot out.'

Southernwood, also called lad's love and old man, is *Artemisia abrotanum*, a fine green-gray ornamental.

Not all of the homely folk beliefs have been discarded in our time even in well-settled districts. Not so many years ago, before we owned an electric refrigerator on our herb farm, we used to buy ice from a New England dairy farmer whose mother was fond of gardening. Every spring she planted her own vegetables, always during the waxing of the moon, for like some of her English forebears, she believed that the planets influenced the work of the gardener.

William Coles, famous herbalist of the seventeenth century, wrote in his *Art of Simpling,* 'the full Moon is a good time to gather those herbs in, out of which the juyce is to be taken, for then are they most plentifully stored therewith.'

Coles defined simpling as the 'Art which teacheth the knowledge of all Druggs and Physicall Ingredients, but especially of Plants, their Divisions, Definitions, Differences, Descriptions, Places, Names, Times, Vertues, Uses, Temperature, and Signatures.'

During the seventeenth century the curious Doctrine of Signatures was a popular theory, and as Coles explains, 'The Mercy of God—hath not only stamped upon them [herbs] a distinct forme, but also given them particular Signatures, whereby a Man may read, even in legible Characters, the use of them.' The theory is best made clear by an example. 'That Plant that is called Adder's Tongue, because the stalke of it represents one,' says Coles, 'is a soveraigne wound Herbe to cure the biting of an Adder, or any other venemous Creature.' Medicine was indeed simple in the days when men believed in the Doctrine of Signatures.

Another seventeenth-century physician and author, Nicholas Culpeper, 'Student in physic and astrology,' is famous or infamous, depending upon whether or not the reader believes in astrology. Culpeper was called an old rogue by one modern herbalist, and, in his own time, was denounced by the college of physicians. Nevertheless, this astrologer-physician was popular with many of his contemporaries and during his lifetime his book was what might now be termed a best seller. Today he is of great interest to those who believe in looking up to the stars for guidance, and at least amusing to those who claim that astrology is a superstition.

Culpeper maintained that 'The admirable Harmony of the Creation' could be seen in 'the influence of Stars upon Herbs and the Body of Man.' In order to cure disease, the sufferer must first consider 'what planet causeth the disease,' then 'by what planet the afflicted part of the body is governed,' so that the afflicted person could fight disease by 'Herbs of the planet, opposite to the planet that causes' the disease; or, contrarily, some diseases could be cured by 'Sympathy,' that is, by the planet that governed the disease, 'As the Sun and the Moon by their Herbs cure the Eyes.'

For a random note from Culpeper, take this passage on rosemary. 'The sun claims privilege in it, and it is under the celestial Ram. It helpeth a weak memory and quickeneth the senses.' This is the rosemary to use in the kitchen with fish, pork, and roast beef.

But it was only during certain periods that the herbalists consulted the planets. Looking back once more to rosemary, herb of remembrance, we meet this excellent aromatic herb when Dioscorides mentions it as an herb used, like the true laurel, for crowning victors. As he explains, 'they which plait crowns use it.'

Familiar, too, to us are many other plants described by the great Greek herbalist: fennel, caraway, dill, anise, cumin, coriander, and celery, to mention but a few. As we glance through the ancient Herbal, and other old herb and gardening books, again and again we recognize the herbs we all know today. The old herbals, many of them first editions with fine steel engravings and woodcuts, may be consulted in libraries that specialize in horticultural literature, but almost anyone can go to his own book shelf for an ancient book that contains references to herbs, the Bible.

'But woe unto you, Pharisees! for ye tithe mint and rue and all manner of herbs, and pass over judgment and the love of God.' Luke 11:42.

In the Song of Solomon, we read of costly saffron which is made of the dried stigmas of *Crocus sativus*, the pretty little fall-blooming crocus which you can grow in your herb garden. Again, in Matthew 23:23, we are admonished, 'Woe unto you, scribes and Pharisees, hypocrites! for ye pay tithe of mint and anise and cummin, and have omitted the weightier *matters* of the law, judgment, mercy, and faith.'

There are mistakes in the identification of some plants in the Bible, errors made by scholars of long ago who had not seen the Holy Land. Modern authorities * say that the 'Lilies of the field' were not true lilies but probably poppy anemones, and also that the anise in the quotation above was not anise but probable dill. But the mint was a species that is known in modern gardens and the cumin was the kind grown today, and so too were other biblical herbs, such as coriander, mustard, garlic, and the green bay tree.

Herbs have a history as old as that of man. They are mentioned in written history not only in the Bible but also in an ancient Egyptian papyrus of 1500 B.C.; we meet them in Shakespeare, in Vergil, and in old manuscripts from monasteries where the art of simpling was practised centuries ago.

The New World

In comparatively recent times, shortly after the first settlements in America were established, there is mention of these ancient herbs. Although the settlers did adopt a few of the native American tea herbs known to the Indians, and also a few of the wild medicinals, most of the herbs they used were

* See Check-List of Plants mentioned in the Bible (based on the work of Dr. H. N. Moldenke), *Journal of the New York Botanical Garden*, March 1941.

brought with them from the Old World; and today a goodly number of the ancient herbs of the Mediterranean region are found in this country as escapes from colonial gardens, and are commonly, but erroneously, believed to be wild.

A record of the European herbs introduced to America in the seventeenth century has been kept in the quaint and fascinating book called *New England's Rarities,* written by John Josselyn, an English gentleman who visited his brother's plantation 'an hundred leagues to the Eastward of Boston,' Massachusetts. John Josselyn's book was first printed in London at the Green Dragon in St. Paul's Church Yard in 1672. Among other things, Josselyn gives a list 'Of such plants as have sprung up since the English Planted and Kept Cattle in New England.' This list includes several of our most disliked weeds: 'Nettlestinging' (still used by gourmets today for nettle soup); dandelions, still enjoyed by us for salads and boiled greens; and that pest of pests, but an honorable old medicinal herb, the 'plaintain,' unwanted today even by the most fanatical herb gardener.

Perhaps of more interest is Josselyn's list 'Of such Garden Herbs—as do thrive there [in Massachusetts], and of such as do not.' Among those that are hardy, he speaks of spearmint, lavender cotton (santolina), pennyroyal, smalledge (lovage), anise, coriander, and dill. 'Fetherfew [feverfew] prospereth exceedingly,' but 'Southernwood is no Plant for this Country, Nor Rosemary, Nor Bayes.' In our experience, southernwood is very hardy, but when the frosts are due, we too, like the early settlers, must bring in rosemary and bay.

Some of the early herb plantings in the New World were 'yarb' patches at the kitchen door; others were knot gardens in the tradition then popular in England; still others were elaborate mazes, with box and yew, also popular in the sixteenth and seventeenth centuries. About 1700 the parterre became fashionable.

The kitchen garden at Mount Vernon was restored in 1936 from descriptions in George Washington's diary, other writings by him, and 'books which the General owned and used.' Among the herbs known to have been planted in the original garden and grown today as edging plants in this restored colonial kitchen garden are: *

Balm, Lemon	Lavender
Basil	Mint
Bergamot	Pennyroyal
Catnip	Rosemary
Fennel, Sweet	Rue
Germander	Santolina
Hyssop	

In the flower garden at Mount Vernon, there are restorations of two parterres of dwarf boxwood believed to have been developed by the General's gardener during the last decade of the eighteenth century.

Now having followed the history of herbs, however briefly, through the ages and mentioned some of their common uses in former times, it seems appropriate to end on a 'modern' note, written in the year 1699. We refer to a book by John Evelyn, a contemporary of Pepys, but, nevertheless, a very modern man in some ways. In the *Acetaria, a Discourse of Sallets,* he discusses the merits of some seventy-three salad plants, especially the 'crude sallets,' the uncooked greens and vegetables he himself liked for 'salleting.'

John Evelyn was a vegetarian. He cites the 'short lives of most Carnivorous Animals, compared with the Grass Feeders, and the Ruminating kind; as the Hart, Camel, and the longaevous Elephant, and other feeders on Roots and Vegetables,' but of more importance, he has some admirable suggestions for a modern salad bowl. Not only does he give ideas for literally bushels of 'sallets,' but also he explains how beneficial each single plant is to the person who eats it. For example, of tarragon—most commonly used today for making salad vinegar—he says that 'the tops and young Shoots' are never to be left out of salads, and we agree, 'especially where there is much Lettuce. Tis highly cordial and friendly to the Head, Heart, Liver.'

* Courtesy of The Mount Vernon Ladies' Association of the Union, Mount Vernon, Virginia.

When modern physicians have further studied the effects of tarragon and other herbs upon the human body, we believe that many of the remedies of the old physicians will be proved beneficial. Until then we shall continue to enjoy certain recommendations of the ancients that help make our cooking 'highly cordial and friendly' to the head and the heart as well as to our digestion.

THE VIRTUES OF KITCHEN HERBS

As we have pointed out, a common kitchen herb, such as parsley, was used formerly not for its flavor alone but for the good it would do one's health, and other kitchen herbs were recommended for various troubles, for the good of man's stomach, his head, or his 'joynts,' or to bolster his courage, or protect him from the plague or the devil. Each kind had its own inherent virtue, for in days gone by there was no strict division between medicinal and culinary herbs, and sweet herbs and potherbs were prescribed. There follow some random notes for the modern cook who, while seasoning food with herbs, likes to know a little of the ancient kitchen folklore.

Angelica

This herb is said to have its name from its 'angelic' healing qualities. It was 'Soveraigne' against the plague, according to Coles who wrote, in the seventeenth century, *The Art of Simpling*. It was good for the heart, and, if carried on the person, would ward off witches.

Anise

Anise was recommended by Dioscorides of Greece for headaches.

Balm, Lemon

The virtue of lemon balm used as a washing water, according to the English physician, Parkinson (1629), was 'to comfort the veines and sinewes' in the summer time. Quite similarly in Greece, in the first century of the Christian era, the leaves of lemon balm '—with salt—being smeared on, they asuuage ye pains of ye goutie.'

Basil

The virtues of basil are disputed. In India it is a sacred herb. In Italy, basil means love and sympathy; to the Greeks, hate. Or as the Englishman, Culpeper, aptly stated, 'This is the herb which all authors are together by the ears about, and rail at one another (like lawyers).'

Bay, Sweet

The sweet bay tree, renowned as the victor's crown, was also known as a medicinal herb. Dioscorides stated that bay leaves 'being layd on with barly flour and bread' were 'of force to assuage any inflammations.' Some centuries later, Culpeper, in England (1652), said that bay 'resists witchcraft very potently.'

Borage

Borage
Brings always courage.

In ancient times when a knight set out on a crusade, a borage flower was floated in his stirrup cup.

Burnet, Salad

In ancient Greece the leaves were used to help heal wounds.
Culpeper says, burnet 'is a most precious little herb,—the continual use of it preserves the body in health, and the spirits in vigor—'
And Parkinson, 'put a few leaves in a cup of claret wine— to help make the heart merrie.'

Caraway

Caraway was recommended in Greece as long ago as the first century of the Christian era for good digestion.

Chervil

Famous in Continental kitchens (particularly in France) as one of the important herbs in 'Omelette aux fines herbes,' there seem to be few references to medicinal uses of this herb. The chervil known to the ancients is sweet cicely.

Chicory

Known to John Evelyn, the 'sallet' lover, as Succory, was by him considered 'more grateful to the Stomach than the Palate.'

Chives (See Onions)

Cicely, Sweet

According to Culpeper, 'The root boiled, and eaten with oil and vinegar (or without oil) do much please and warm old and cold stomachs oppressed with wind or phlegm, or those that have the phthisic or consumption of the lungs.'

In ancient Greece it was recommended to bring immunity in 'pestilentiall seasons.' 'Drink twice or thrice a day with wine.' (Dioscorides.)

Coriander

Long known as a vermifuge. Dioscorides said that it 'heals ye Erysipelata and creeping ulcers.'

Costmary

'A wonderful help to all sorts of dry agues,—astringent and strengthens the liver, and all other inward parts.' (Culpeper, 1652.)

Cress, Upland

We were unable to identify upland cress in the old herbal manuscripts but Dioscorides lists peppergrass (*Lepidium sativum*) as an aphrodisiac.

Dill

Dioscorides stated that dill would 'stayeth ye hickets,—' (hiccups). According to Culpeper, dill would strengthen the brain. And in the writings of Parkinson, King's herbalist and seventeenth-century apothecary, we came across notations on dill that sound strikingly like our own. Dill 'is put among pickled cowcumbers, wherewith it doth well agree, gluing into the cold fruit a pretty spicie taste or rellish.' And 'The leaves of Dill are much used in some places with Fish, as they doe Fennell.'

Fennel

'Juice of the bruised stalks, and ye leaves being dried in ye sun,' made a good eye medicine. (Dioscorides.) It was also considered good for stomach and bladder troubles.

Garlic

In ancient Greece this 'sharp herb' was said to be 'good as none other thing, for such as are bitten of vipers—' Also used medicinally in Greece, Egypt, China, and Rome.

The great 'sallet' maker, John Evelyn (1699), said, 'To be sure, 'tis not for Ladies palats, nor for those who court them, further than to permit a light touch on the Dish, with a Clove thereof.'

Rocombole, giant garlic, is recommended by Dioscorides.

Hops

Long considered a good medicine for the spleen. Also, the dried catkins were used for making pillows for easing neuralgia.

Horehound

In Dioscorides' day 'The dry leaves of this, with ye seed being sodden with water, or juiced when green, is given with honey to ye phthisicall asthmaticall, and to such as cough.' Horehound candy is still made in this country for the same purpose.

Horse-Radish

This hot member of the mustard family has long been considered good for digestion and as a stimulant for the appetite. William Coles in *The Art of Simpling,* printed at the Angell in Cornhill, London, 1657, says, 'Horseradish root sliced thin with a little vinegar is a wholesome sauce with Mutton.'

Hyssop

Parkinson, the King's herbalist, prescribed 'pils' made of hyssop with horehound, castor, and peony roots 'for the Falling sicknesse [epilepsy].'

Lovage

The seeds of lovage were formerly used medicinally for the 'Falling sicknesse.' The juices were also used in witches' ointment.

Marigold, Pot (*Calendula*)

The blossoms of this common garden flower were formerly thought to be effective in removing warts. They were also believed to be good for heart trouble.

Marjoram, Sweet

John Gerard, the King's herbalist in sixteenth-century England, says sweet marjoram 'is a remedie against cold diseases of the braine and head, being taken anyway to your best liking.' He also recommends it for people who are 'given to over-much sighing.'

Mint

John Gerard (1597) recommends mint. 'Garden Mints taken in meate or drinke warmeth and strengtheneth the stomache— and causeth good digestion.' Parkinson, a few years later, also recommends mint for weak stomachs.

Mustard

A tonic potherb in Dioscorides' time.

Nasturtiums

Nasturtiums were formerly thought to purge the brain and quicken the spirit.

Onions (including chives, shallots, top onions, etc.)

'The Oynion was inviting to the appetite,' and considered 'good for the belly.' (Dioscorides.)

Orach

This medicinal potherb is a cooling herb, and boiled without any water but its own moisture, it was said, at one time, to be good for the womb.

Origanum

In Greece it was taken for 'ye convulsions, and rupture, and dropsies.' (Dioscorides.) It was used also as a strewing herb in the belief that it expelled serpents.

Parsley

Parsley was as popular in old England as it is today in America, both with meats and as a garnish.

Parkinson (1629): 'Parsley is much used in all sorts of meates, both boyled, roasted, fryed, stewed etc. and being greene it serveth to lay upon sundry meates, as beefe, as also onto legges of Mutton, with a little beefe suet among it.' The ancient medicinal 'vertues' of parsley have been noted earlier in this chapter.

Pennyroyal

As we have already pointed out in the beginning of this chapter, pennyroyal has been known since the first century A.D. in Greece as a remedy for indigestion. It was also worn as a garland to prevent 'swimming in the head.'

Rocombole (See Garlic)

Rosemary (See above, in text)

Rhubarb

The roots were prescribed by Dioscorides as a medicinal. Coles recommended rhubarb for stomach, liver, and blood.

Rue

'Being eaten beforehand ye leaves by themselves, or with Wallnuts, or with dry figs, it makes poisons ineffectual.' (Dioscorides.) Dioscorides praised rue as a medicine 'for coughs, inflammations of the lungs—ye griefs of ye hips, or ye joints.'

Saffron

Coles, 1657, *The Art of Simpling,* said that saffron 'strengthens the Heart exceedingly, quickneth the Braine, helps consumptions of the Lungs.' Dioscorides said it was an aphrodisiac.

There is a romantic legend that saffron was first brought into England in a crusader's staff.

Sage

Sage has been known for centuries as an important health herb. There is an old English proverb.

> He who would live for aye
> Must eat Sage in May.

Samphire

Dioscorides recommended samphire as a medicinal potherb.

Savory

In early days in England, savory was considered an herb good for digestion.

Shallots (See Onions)

Skirret

According to John Evelyn, the old potherb skirret was 'good for the stomach, exceedingly nourishing, wholesome and delicate; of all the Root-kind, not subject to be windy, and so valued by the Emperor Tiberius, that he accepted them for Tribute.'

Tansy

A vermifuge, a strewing herb, a stomachic—all these virtues were recognized in tansy in colonial times. Coles, *The Art of Simpling* (1657), gives this recipe: 'I have heard that if Maids will take wilde Tansy, and lay it to sod in Buttermilke for the space of nine dayes, and wash their faces therewith, it will make them look very faire.'

Tarragon

Tarragon seems not to have been used much in medieval times, but was well recommended by John Evelyn, the 'sallet' maker of seventeenth-century England. (See above.)

Thyme

Thyme, like sage, has been known for centuries for its virtues. Thyme with honey, said John Gerard, is 'good against the cough and shortnesse of the breath—' Parkinson declared it was.

'a speciall helpe to melancholicke and spleneticke diseases—' He also suggested thyme in 'pils for the head and stomach.' The oil of thyme was for soothing an aching tooth.

Woodruff, Sweet

Long considered good for the heart.

Conclusion

Vinegar of the Four Thieves: Take the tops of Sea and Roman Wormwood, Rosemary, Sage, Mint and Rue, of each an ounce and a half; Lavender Flowers, two ounces, Calamus Aromaticus, Cinnamon, Cloves, Nutmeg, and Garlic, of each a quarter of an ounce; Camphire, half an ounce, Red Wine Vinegar, a gallon.

The quotation above, from the eighteenth-century publication, *The Toilet of Flora,* gives an indication of the faith then shared by all, including even members of the underworld, in the virtues of herbs. The four thieves believed that this herb wine vinegar was so potent, and the protective powers so strong, that it would immunize them against infection from the great plague while they robbed the bodies of people who had died of the disease.

Most people in the twentieth century agree that prescriptions both for the protective or, as they are called today, the preventive medicines, and for the curative medicines should be left to modern physicians and pharmacists. Yet, though modern readers regard with amusement some of the old recipes for herbal remedies, there is more real medicine in herbs than anyone who is inexperienced in this field may realize. Aside from the hocus-pocus of old herbal lore, there remains the indisputable fact that the flavor and fragrance of herbs which were valued in past centuries are also a tonic for people today. Delectable herb vinegars and fresh green herbs in salads and other culinary preparations, dried herbs as seasoning for ragouts and similar oven dishes, all make food so palatable that the appetite is stimulated, enjoyment in eating is fostered, and the health is subsequently improved.

And for one who has a garden, there is 'protective medicine' in growing herbs for his own use. The person who has not yet had the experience of walking in a garden of herbs can scarcely imagine the pleasure of working among aromatic plants. In addition to the beauty of growing herbs, each leaf that is touched, each stem that is broken, each small plant that is crushed underfoot gives forth a distinctive fragrance which, during harvest time, is multiplied into a blend of essences, a truly heady aroma.

In short, the modern gardener who applies up-to-date horti-cultural methods to his garden and uses the harvest with intelli-gent selection will find that the labor involved seems more festive than laborious, and very likely he will soon believe, as did his forebears, in the inherent 'vertues' of herbs.

Appendix

REGIONAL DATA

In gathering material on the growing of herbs, we solicited information from authorities all over the United States and Canada—colleges of agriculture and pharmacy, botany departments in state universities, state agricultural experiment stations, botanical gardens, and historic herb gardens. We found that despite a wide variation in climate, a surprisingly large number of the herbs that do well in our New England garden grow equally well in the North Central states and Quebec, in the South and on the Great Plains, in the Rocky Mountain states and on the Pacific coast. Some other herbs are less adaptable. There is not space here to give details on each species, and for help on the problem of geographic limitations, we suggest you consult the herb garden nearest you, as listed elsewhere in the appendix. We intend only to summarize briefly the advantages herb growers enjoy in certain areas and a few of the difficulties they encounter, urging the herb grower to bear in mind the necessity for good soil, good drainage, plenty of sunshine (usually), and the fact that local climatic conditions due to altitude, prevailing winds, and other factors may affect an individual garden to such an extent that it does not fit into any generalization for the area.

ZONE 1: THE NORTHEAST

The Northeast (United States) has an excellent climate for growing herbs and the one limitation, particularly in the more northerly parts, is the cold winter climate. A tender annual herb such as sesame must be started in a greenhouse to assure maturity in New England. Obviously an herb such as sweet bay can be kept in the garden during the summer months only and some other perennials must be treated as annuals or given winter cover in this zero and sub-zero region, as indicated in the text.

Barring a year of severe drought, there is little complaint of lack of moisture for growing herbs in the Northeast. An exception is found in one of the most beautiful and famous herb gardens, the Cloisters in New York City. During the summer months the sun beating against the massive stone walls combined with drying winds creates a hot, dry situation that almost simulates the desert, and here the herb garden must be watered regularly.

Zone 2: The Southeast

All of the herbs listed in the text, with one exception, grow very well in the vicinity of Williamsburg, Virginia. The winter climate in this region is too cool for sweet bay. Many of these same herbs are known to do well in the vicinity of Charleston, South Carolina, and Chapel Hill, North Carolina, although around Chapel Hill an herb such as rhubarb does poorly, probably because of the heat.

In the more tropical parts of the Southeast, particularly Florida, it is customary to grow some of the annuals during the winter months. In the vicinity of Gainesville, Florida, herbs among the basic twenty-four that grow well are sweet basil, borage, dill, nasturtiums, parsley, and summer savory (annuals and biennials); and lemon balm, salad burnet, chives, garlic, sweet marjoram, spearmint, origanum, rosemary, and garden thyme (perennials). Some annuals such as sesame which are tender plants when grown in the Northeast, do well here. Among the perennials—other than the basic ones listed in this book—that are grown successfully are germander, santolina, betony, and top onions. Some perennials—aconite, autumn crocus, hop vine, lavender, orris—do not grow well in this section because of the heat.

Zone 3: North Central

The North Central states have an excellent climate for growing the most important commercial herb in the United States, namely, mint. The soil in Ohio, Indiana, and Michigan is particularly well adapted for this herb and also for many others. A report from Wooster, Ohio, shows that the basic twenty-four and nearly all of the other herbs listed in this book, with bayberry the exception, do well in this vicinity, though the herb grower must keep in mind of course the fact that a tender perennial such as rosemary cannot be left in the garden during winter. Perennials such as chives, origanum, sage, garden thyme, horehound, and orris—to mention only a few—and annuals such as dill and coriander are known to do well in the vicinity of Purdue University, Indiana. A report from Hammond, Indiana, indicates that perennials such as garlic and shallots grow poorly in this region, probably because the soil is too cool; garden thyme and lavender (*L. vera*) are not winter hardy; and lemon balm needs winter cover except when the snow is heavy.

A report from the more southerly region of the North Central states indicates, as would be expected, that heat rather than cold is a limiting factor in growing some herbs. In the vicinity of Lexington, Kentucky, the growing season is too hot for an annual such as pot marigold. Perennials such as sweet cicely, costmary, origanum, English pennyroyal, lovage—also saffron and skirret—and annuals such as orach and roquette do well, but it is not a good climate for bayberry, and some other perennials such as winter savory, sweet woodruff, germander, and tarragon die out.

Zone 4: Northern Plains

Our report for this zone is from Brookings, South Dakota. Here the perennials among the basic twenty-four herbs, lemon balm, salad burnet, chives, costmary, garlic, lovage, sweet marjoram, spearmint, origanum, English pennyroyal, rosemary, sage, tarragon, and thyme, and annuals and biennials, sweet basil, borage, chervil, dill, nasturtiums, parsley are known to grow well. Many other perennials listed in the book, such as aconite and horehound, and annuals such as pot marigold and safflower, to mention a few, also do well. The chief limiting factor in growing herbs at Brookings seems to be the same as for New England, namely, severe winter weather. The more tender perennials such as rosemary have to be wintered indoors, of course, and some others need winter cover.

Zone 5: Central Plains

The report for this zone, from St. Louis, Missouri, shows that the perennials among the basic twenty-four, lemon balm, chives, costmary, garlic, lovage, rosemary, sweet marjoram, spearmint, sage, shallots, and garden thyme, and the annuals and biennials, sweet basil, borage, cress, dill, summer savory, and many other perennials such as hyssop and aconite, and annuals such as orach and sesame do well here. The winter climate is too cold for rosemary to remain out of doors but the major limitation in growing some other herbs here is due not to the winter but to the summer climate, which is hot and dry. Because of heat, lavender (*L. vera*) and violets do only fairly well, and heat and drought cause chervil, sweet cicely, lovage, and English penny-royal to grow poorly.

Zone 6: Southern Plains

Our report for this zone comes from Austin, Texas, where, among the twenty-four basic herbs, the perennials, lemon balm, salad burnet, chives, garlic, sweet marjoram, spearmint, origa-num, rosemary, sage, shallots, and garden thyme, and the an-nuals, sweet basil, borage, dill, nasturtiums, summer savory, grow well. Many other perennials such as horehound and laven-der, and annuals such as sesame and caraway also do well, but the climate is too hot for herbs such as anise, chicory, tarragon, and rhubarb; too dry for American pennyroyal; and too hot and dry for aconite, autumn crocus, and bergamot.

Zone 7: Northwest Coastal

This area includes some of the richest commercial mint-producing land in America. The Yakima Valley of Washington and the Willamette Valley of Oregon and other parts of the Pacific Northwest have an excellent climate for growing mint and many other herbs. Several hundred species and varieties, including all but one (samphire has not been tested) listed in this book, are grown successfully in the vicinity of Seattle, Washington. The climate here is so mild that even the sweet bay is left in the garden all year around and does very well except during an exceptionally cold winter when the temperature may drop to nearly zero. During such a season, *Laurus nobilis* dies to the roots or is completely winterkilled.

Zone 8: Northwest Mountains

We have a report from the vicinity of Missoula, Montana, in the Rocky Mountain region, where the average temperature during the month of July is 67° F. and the January average, 23° F. Among the twenty-four basic herbs that have been tested and do well here are the perennials, lovage, spearmint, and sage, and the annual, dill. Other perennials known to grow well here are aconite, chamomile, horehound, orris, pyrethrum, and wormwood, and the annuals, anise, caraway, coriander, and safflower. True lavender (*L. vera*) does not do well in this area, but *L. spicata* does very well. Many other herbs would undoubtedly grow well in this zone if they were tried.

Zone 9: Southwest Coastal

Coastal California is well known for its excellent climate for growing herbs. Elsewhere in the appendix we have listed eight herb gardens open to the public in this rich agricultural area, in places as far apart as San Francisco and Santa Barbara.

A report from the vicinity of Los Angeles on the specific herbs listed in this book indicates that most of them grow with excellent or good results and nearly all the others will grow satisfactorily with reasonable care. The perennials, rosemary and garden sage, and the biennial clary sage do best here in full sun in a dry situation, while perennials such as tarragon and tansy and the biennial angelica do best in semi-shade. Chives and parsley both need a great deal of water. Anise, caraway, chervil, cumin, and coriander do not thrive in mid-summer heat, going to seed too fast, and the results with a few others such as autumn crocus, saffron crocus, and lovage are uncertain.

Zone 10: The Southwest
(Inland)

Most of this area has a very arid, semi-desert, or desert, climate, and here herbs, like most other crops, must be raised under irrigation. In the warmer sections, some herbs do best when cultivated in patio gardens during the winter months. We have a specific report from the vicinity of Tucson, Arizona, where the following perennials have been grown successfully: catnip, lovage, columbine, orris, pyrethrum, rhubarb, kazanlik rose, rosemary, sage, spearmint, and violets. Among the annuals grown successfully here are coriander, dill, fennel, pot marigold, and safflower. Anise does fairly well.

Zone 11: Eastern Canada

All of the herbs listed in this book with the exception of *Artemisia pontica* have been tested and grown successfully in the vicinity of Montreal, but some of the perennials which are hardy in many areas in the northern parts of the states are treated as annuals or wintered indoors and propagated annually from cuttings. Although a few of these might live over the winter with cover, it is easier to keep a plant or two indoors for propagation purposes, or to sow seeds each spring.

Among the twenty-four basic herbs, the perennials, sweet cicely, chives, costmary, lovage, spearmint, origanum, English pennyroyal, sage, shallots, and tarragon, are reported to be hardy. Among those not reliably hardy are lemon balm, which is propagated annually from cuttings, salad burnet, which is raised annually from seeds, and sweet marjoram and garden thyme, which are propagated annually from cuttings or seeds. Garlic bulbs are wintered in the cellar and replanted in the spring; rosemary is wintered indoors. Among the other perennials listed in this book, rue, winter savory, and santolina are propagated annually from cuttings, and lavender and pyrethrum and, of course, sweet bay, like rosemary, are wintered indoors. Germander does not winterkill but freezes back, and saffron crocus does not grow very satisfactorily because it flowers too late.

HERB GARDENS

There follows a list (compiled by the author in co-operation with The Herb Society of America) of non-commercial herb gardens in the United States and Canada. These gardens are open to the public and admission is free unless otherwise stated.

UNIVERSITY OF ARIZONA PHARMACY COLLEGE, Tucson, Arizona: *Medicinal plant garden.*

LOS ANGELES STATE AND COUNTY ARBORETUM, 291 N. Old Ranch Road, Arcadia, California: *Herb garden and medicinal plant garden in planning stage.*

UNIVERSITY OF CALIFORNIA BOTANICAL GARDEN, Berkeley, California: *Medicinal herb garden, culinary herb garden.*

STEVENSON HOUSE STATE HISTORICAL MONUMENT, 530 Houston Street, Monterey, California: *Culinary and medicinal herbs of early California.*

MILLS COLLEGE, Oakland, California: *Herb garden* (by appointment).

MARIN ART AND GARDEN CENTER, Ross, California: *Culinary and medicinal herbs.*

HUNTINGTON BOTANICAL GARDEN, Oxford and Stratford Roads, San Marino, California: *Herb plantings with other plants.*

STRYBING ARBORETUM AND BOTANIC GARDEN, McLaren Lodge, Golden Gate Park, San Francisco, California: *Medicinal plant garden.*

SANTA BARBARA BOTANIC GARDEN, Santa Barbara, California: *Native California herbs and medicinal plants among other plants.*

HENRY WHITFIELD HOUSE HERB GARDEN, Henry Whitfield State Historical Museum, Guilford, Connecticut: *Restricted to herbs in this country by 1639 and some native herbs.*

STORRS EXPERIMENT STATION UNIVERSITY OF CONNECTICUT HERB GARDEN, North Coventry, Connecticut.

Pharmacy Garden, University of Connecticut, Storrs, Connecticut.

The Cottage Herb Garden, Washington Cathedral, Washington, D. C.: *Biblical herb garden, Shakespearean herb garden, and many culinary herbs.*

Medicinal Plant Garden, College of Pharmacy, University of Florida, Gainesville, Florida.

Indiana Botanic Gardens, 626 177th Street, Hammond, Indiana: *Herb garden, medicinal plant garden, herbs used by American Indians.*

J. I. Holcomb Gardens, Butler University, Indianapolis, Indiana: *Medicinal plant garden in planning stage.*

Medicinal Plant Garden, School of Pharmacy, Purdue University, West Lafayette, Indiana.

Garden at Ashland, Home of Henry Clay, East Main and Sycamore Road, Lexington, Kentucky: *Herb garden in planning stage* (fee for house only).

Concord Antiquarian Society, Lexington Road and Cambridge Turnpike, Concord, Massachusetts: *Herb garden, some medicinal plants. A Garden of Fragrances* ($.35 adults, $.20 children).

Massachusetts College of Pharmacy, Jamaica Plain, Massachusetts: *Herb garden, medicinal plant garden.*

Lee Mansion Herb Garden, Bank Square, Marblehead, Massachusetts: *Herbs for a household of* 1768 (fee $.50 for house and none for garden).

The Botanic Garden of Smith College, Northampton, Massachusetts: *Herb garden.*

Berkshire Garden Center, Stockbridge, Massachusetts: *Herb garden on terrace.*

Parson Capen House, 1 Hawlett Street, Topsfield, Massachusetts: *Herb garden* (fee $.25).

Grandmother's Garden, Westfield, Massachusetts: *Herb garden, medicinal, culinary, fragrant.*

AN HERB GARDEN CALLED AUNT HELEN'S GARDEN, Storrowton, Eastern States Exposition Grounds, West Springfield, Massachusetts.

GARDEN OF THE LEAVENED HEART, Greenfield Village, Dearborn, Michigan: *Herb garden, medicinal plant garden* (fee included in admission to village).

BEAL-GARFIELD BOTANICAL GARDEN, Michigan State College, East Lansing, Michigan: *Economic plant garden; fiber plants, dye stuffs, essential oil plants, etc.* 12 *large beds devoted to herbs, drug and medicinal plants.*

MISSOURI BOTANICAL GARDEN, 2315 Tower Grove Ave., St. Louis 10, Missouri: *Herb garden.*

WASHINGTON UNIVERSITY HERB GARDEN, Henry Shaw School of Botany, Washington University, St. Louis 5, Missouri.

PHARMACY DRUG GARDEN, Montana State University, Missoula, Montana: *Medicinal plant garden* (not open to public).

TEN BROECK-OLCOTT MANSION (1798), Albany, New York: *Herb garden; geometrical design.*

NEW YORK STATE HISTORICAL ASSOCIATION, Cooperstown, New York: FENIMORE HOUSE, *Medicinal herbs, first quarter nineteenth century* (admission free); THE FARMER'S MUSEUM, *Medicinal herbs* (admission $.75).

BROOKLYN BOTANIC GARDEN, 1000 Washington Ave., Brooklyn 25, New York: *Elizabethan knot garden, Shakespeare garden, culinary and medicinal herbs.*

THE NEW YORK BOTANICAL GARDEN, Bronx Park, New York 58, New York: *Herb garden* (free except Saturday, Sunday, and holidays).

MEDIEVAL HERB GARDEN IN THE GARDEN COURT OF BONNEFONT CLOISTER, *The Cloisters,* Branch of the Metropolitan Museum of Art, Fort Tryon Park, New York, New York.

THORNDEN PARK HERB GARDEN, Thornden Park, Syracuse, New York: *Culinary and medicinal; knot gardens.*

DRUG PLANT GARDEN, c/o North Carolina Pharmaceutical Research Foundation, School of Pharmacy, University of North Carolina,

Chapel Hill, North Carolina: *Herb garden, medicinal plant garden; located on Mason Farm, a tract of 1900 acres.*

SCHOOL OF PHARMACY, North Dakota Agricultural College, Fargo, North Dakota: *Medicinal plant garden.*

CLEVELAND FINE ARTS GARDEN AND CULTURAL GARDENS, 213 City Hall, Cleveland, Ohio: *Herb garden, medicinal plant garden, Shakespeare garden, cultural gardens of many different nations.*

WADE PARK HERB GARDEN, Wade Park, Cleveland, Ohio: *Knot garden, beds of medicinal, culinary, seed, and fragrance herbs.*

MEDICINAL PLANT GARDEN, College of Pharmacy, The Ohio State University, Columbus, Ohio.

HERB GARDEN IN FIRESTONE GARDENS, Ohio Agricultural Experiment Station, Wooster, Ohio.

GARDEN FOR THE BLIND, The John J. Tyler Arboretum, Lima, Delaware County, Pennsylvania: *Culinary herbs, planted for fragrance and texture; all plants are marked in Braille.*

HERB GARDEN AT CEDAR GROVE, Fairmount Park, Philadelphia, Pennsylvania: *Historical setting* (fee for house).

KILMER BOTANICAL GARDEN, Philadelphia College of Pharmacy and Science, 43rd Street, and Kingsessing and Woodland Aves., Philadelphia 4, Pennsylvania: *Medicinal plant garden.*

MEDICINAL HERB GARDEN, College of Physicians of Philadelphia, 19 South 22nd Street, Philadelphia, Pennsylvania.

UNIVERSITY OF PITTSBURGH SCHOOL OF PHARMACY MEDICINAL PLANT GARDEN, Schenley Park, Pittsburgh 13, Pennsylvania.

RHODE ISLAND COLLEGE OF PHARMACY AND ALLIED SCIENCES, 235 Benefit Street, Providence, Rhode Island: *Herb garden, medicinal plant garden.*

THE HEYWARD-WASHINGTON GARDEN, 87 Church Street, Charleston, South Carolina: *Herb garden, knot garden* (admission $.50 includes admission to house built *c.* 1760).

MRS. W. C. COLEMAN, 14 Claremore Ave., Greenville, South Carolina: *Collection of herbs.*

HORTICULTURE GARDEN, MEDICINAL PLANT GARDEN, South Dakota State College, Brookings, South Dakota: *Herb garden, medicinal plants.*

COLLEGE OF PHARMACY DRUG GARDEN, University of Texas, Austin, Texas: *Herb garden, medicinal plant garden* (phone in advance).

MOUNT VERNON KITCHEN GARDEN, The Mount Vernon Ladies' Association of the Union, Mount Vernon, Virginia: *A typical colonial kitchen garden, including herbs; parterres* (admission $.50).

COLONIAL STYLE GARDEN, GEORGE WASHINGTON BIRTHPLACE NATIONAL MONUMENT, Washington's Birthplace, Westmoreland County, Virginia (National Park Service; U. S. Department of the Interior): *Herb garden with culinary and medicinal herbs used during the eighteenth century, or earlier.*

THE HERB GARDEN, Stratford Hall, Westmoreland County, Virginia (Robert E. Lee Memorial Foundation): *Herbs included in small garden enclosed by original (1729) brick wall behind old outside kitchen* (admission to house and garden $.50).

(1) JOHN BLAIR HERB GARDEN, (2) WYTHE HERB GARDEN, Colonial Williamsburg, Williamsburg, Virginia: *Simple parterres, culinary and medicinal herbs in both gardens* (John Blair garden free; Wythe garden admission charge).

DRUG PLANT GARDEN, University of Washington, Seattle 5, Washington: *Herb garden, medicinal plant garden; about 5 acres, highly cultivated; symmetrical arrangements; several hundred species and varieties.*

WEST VIRGINIA UNIVERSITY ARBORETUM AND PLANTATIONS, Morgantown, West Virginia: *Medicinal plant garden.*

BOTANICAL GARDEN, University of British Columbia, Vancouver, British Columbia: *Herb garden.*

MONTREAL BOTANICAL GARDEN, 4101 Sherbrooke Street East, Montreal, Canada: *Herb garden, medicinal plant garden.*

SCHOOL OF GARDENING, Niagara Parks Commission, Niagara Falls, Ontario, Canada: *Collection of herbs.*

MEDICINAL PLANT GARDEN, College of Pharmacy, University of Puerto Rico, Rio Piedras, Puerto Rico: *Medicinal plants.*

A SELECTED BIBLIOGRAPHY

The following brief list of books includes general garden reference books of value to the herb grower.

OLD HERBALS AND GARDENING BOOKS

A few are available only in the original in libraries specializing in botanical literature. Reprints of some are on the market today and others may be found in second-hand bookstores.

1779 *The Toilet of Flora,* anonymous. J. Murray, London. Old cosmetic recipes. 'A Collection of the most Simple and Approved Methods of Preparing Baths, Essences, Pomatums [cold creams], Perfumes and Sweet-Scented Waters.'

Reprint, Mrs. Rosetta E. Clarkson, Milford, Connecticut, 1939.

1699 *Acetaria, A Discourse of Sallets,* John Evelyn. Printed for B. Tooke at the Middle-Temple Gate in Fleetstreet, London. Seventy-three kinds of potherbs, fresh greens, and flowers to use in making salads; also information on dressings, and so on.

Reprint, the Women's Auxiliary, Brooklyn Botanic Garden, Brooklyn, New York, 1937.

1672 *New England's Rarities,* John Josselyn. G. Widdowes at the Green Dragon in St. Paul's Church Yard, London. Describes early inhabitants of Massachusetts, early Boston architecture, discoveries in birds, beasts, fishes, serpents, as well as herbs.

Reprint, William Veazie, Boston, 1865.

1657 *The Art of Simpling,* William Coles. London, printed by F. G. for Nath: Brook at the Angell in Cornhill. The time to harvest plants, their 'vertues,' etc.

Reprint, Mrs. Rosetta E. Clarkson, Milford, Connecticut, 1938.

1652 *The Complete Herbal,* Nicholson Culpeper, M.D. London. Old medicinal and occult qualities of herbs.

Reprint, with illustrations in color, Thomas Kelly, Paternoster Row, London, 1850.

1629   *Paradisi in Sole Paradisus Terrestris,* John Parkinson, Apothe-
       cary of London and the King's Herbalist. Humphrey
       Lownes, London. Culinary and medicinal herbs, toilet
       waters, sweet bags, and so forth.

1617   *The Country House-Wives Garden,* William Lawson. London.
       Growing herbs, when to set and sow them; also knots for
       gardens.

       Reprint, Trovillion Private Press, Illinois, 1948.

1597   *The Herball, or Generall Historie of Plantes,* John Gerard,
       Master of Surgery. London. Sixteenth-century uses of herbs.

       Beautifully illustrated with drawings of plants.

First century   *The Greek Herbal,* Dioscorides. Materia Medica com-
       piled during the first century. Illustrated by a Byzantine
       A.D. 512; Englished by John Goodyear, A.D. 1655, the Eng-
       lish translation written in longhand between the lines of
       the Greek text; edited and first printed A.D. 1933 by Robert
       T. Gunther, Oxford University Press, London.

RECENT HERBALS

Clarkson, Rosetta E.
   * *Magic Gardens,* Macmillan, New York, 1939.
   Green Enchantment, Macmillan, New York, 1940.
   Herbs, Their Culture and Uses, Macmillan, New York, 1942.
Fox, Helen M.
   Gardening with Herbs for Flavor and Fragrance, Macmillan,
   New York, 1949.
Freeman, Margaret B.
   Herbs for the Mediaeval Household, The Metropolitan Museum
   of Art, New York, 1943.
Grieve, M.
   * *Modern Herbal,* 2 vols., Harcourt, Brace, New York, 1931.
   * *Culinary Herbs and Condiments,* Harcourt, Brace, New York,
   1934.
Rohde, Eleanour S.
   * *Old English Herbals,* Longmans, Green, London, 1922.
   Herbs and Herb Gardening, reprinted 1948, Medici Society,
   London.

   * Out of print.

Webster, Helen Noyes
    Herbs, How to Grow Them and How to Use Them, revised
    edition, Charles T. Branford, Boston, 1947.

GENERAL GARDEN REFERENCE BOOKS

Bailey, L. H.
    The Standard Cyclopedia of Horticulture, 3 vols., Macmillan,
    New York, 1950. The standard reference book on plants grown
    in the United States and Canada.
Chittenden, Fred J.
    Dictionary of Gardening, 4 vols., Oxford University Press, Lon-
    don, 1952. The modern English encyclopedia, based on Nichol-
    son's *Dictionary of Gardening* but completely revised.
A Symposium (19 authors)
    Hunger Signs in Crops, published by The American Society
    of Agronomy and The National Fertilizer Association, Wash-
    ington, D. C., revised edition 1951. Symptoms of deficiencies in
    plants, with illustrations in color.
The United States Department of Agriculture
    Soils and Men, Yearbook of Agriculture, 1938.
    Insects, Yearbook of Agriculture, 1952.

Index

Figures in bold face refer to pages on which there are illustrations.

24 BASIC HERBS

	BALM, LEMON	BASIL	BORAGE	BURNET	CHERVIL	CHIVES	CICELY, SWEET	COSTMARY	CRESS	DILL	GARLIC	LOVAGE
BEEF	∴			∴	▨	▨		▨	∴	∴	▨	
LAMB	▨			∴	▨	▨			▨	∴▨	▨	
PORK	•	▨			▨	▨			▨	∴		
VEAL	∴				▨	▨				∴	▨	
VENISON					▨						▨	
GOOSE		▨					∴				▨	
STEWS		▨			▨				∴	∴		
FOWL	∴				▨		∴					∴
FISH	▨				▨	∴			▨			▨
SHELL FISH	∴				▨	∴			▨		▨	▨
EGGS	▨				▨	∴						
SALAD	∴	∴	∴	▨	∴	∴	∴		∴	∴	∴	∴
CHOWDER									▨	▨		
CABBAGE				∴	▨	▨				•	•	
PEAS	∴			∴	▨		•					
TOMATO		▨	∴	∴		∴	∴	▨			•	
BEANS					▨							

KEY TO FLAVOR CHART

Diagonal lines mean use herb generously, as much as ½ to 1 teaspoon to a pound or a pint; a full square of diagonal lines means the herb is very sympathetic to the food and can be used in all recipes.